T0302110

International Business and Finance in Japanese Corporations

Recent Harvard-Listed Case Studies and Insights

International Business and Finance in Japanese Corporations

Recent Harvard-Listed Case Studies and Insights

Mitsuru Misawa

University of Hawaii at Manoa, USA

World Scientific

EW JERSEY · LONDON · SINGAPORE · BEIJING · SHANGHAI · HONG KONG · TAIPEI · CHENNAI · TOKYO

Published by

World Scientific Publishing Co. Pte. Ltd.

5 Toh Tuck Link, Singapore 596224

USA office: 27 Warren Street, Suite 401-402, Hackensack, NJ 07601

UK office: 57 Shelton Street, Covent Garden, London WC2H 9HE

Library of Congress Cataloging-in-Publication Data

Names: Misawa, Mitsuru, 1936–   author.

Title: International business and finance in Japanese corporations : recent harvard-listed
    case studies and insights / Mitsuru Misawa, University of Hawaii at Manoa, USA.

Description: New Jersey : World Scientific, [2024] | Includes index.

Identifiers: LCCN 2023021784 | ISBN 9789811277252 (hardcover) |

Subjects: LCSH: Corporations--Japan--Finance. | Industrial management--Japan. |
    Management--Technological innovations. | International business enterprises--Japan.

Classification: LCC HG4245 .M47 2024 | DDC 658.150952--dc23/eng/20230609

LC record available at https://lccn.loc.gov/2023021784

British Library Cataloguing-in-Publication Data

A catalogue record for this book is available from the British Library.

For any available supplementary material, please visit
https://www.worldscientific.com/worldscibooks/10.1142/13436#t=suppl

Desk Editors: Soundararajan Raghuraman/Geysilla Jean

Typeset by Stallion Press
Email: enquiries@stallionpress.com

Printed in Singapore

To my two daughters,
Anne Megumi Misawa and Marie Lei Misawa
And to my two grandchildren,
Madelyn Kimie Wong and Dylan Minghui Misawa Wong

Preface

Since the release of the first and second editions of my previous casebook which contained 20 of my cases on Japanese companies, they have been widely used as both a professional reference and an academic text suitable for upper-level undergraduate or graduate courses at business schools. The objective of this casebook with seven of my new cases is to provide relevant and in-depth information on the current state of business in Japan.

I recently conducted additional case constructions of seven Japanese companies from field studies consisting of numerous visits to and interviews with managers of those corporations. This book contains these seven new cases to reflect the most current changes in the economy that have taken place in Japan since the release of the first and second editions of my previous casebook.

Currently, as the world economy faces serious difficulties, the management of Japanese corporations is attracting attention from all over. Many of these Japanese corporations have been successful in the marketing, production, financing, and allocation of their resources in today's borderless environment. However, these success stories are only partially known in the world.

As shown in this casebook, Japanese businesses have already entered a new era in which they must modify major traditional management practices such as corporate solidarity, homogeneity, and commitment in order to succeed. They must introduce the concepts of individualism and the merit system into their management practices. They must also maintain the advantages of their present legal and regulatory system while at the same time discarding its weak points. They have realized the necessity of shifting away from their conventional system and adopting some new practices. Japanese businesses are aware that the economy can take new steps toward progress only when a new style of Japanese business and legal system are established. Today, Japanese businesses feel the necessity of maintaining their positive assets while at the same time nurturing management techniques oriented toward entrepreneurship and high-technology industries.

In coping with rapid changes in the environment, Japanese management techniques and legal practices continue to change. In the era of internationalization, Japan and foreign countries have followed a path of convergence, despite differing traditions. By following this course, businesses both in Japan and abroad are expected to achieve greater progress in productivity, cost efficiency, and profit maximization, while maintaining good quality control. Professionals must be open-minded in evaluating these techniques and practices, regardless of the source country, and must try to be both flexible and aggressive in experimenting with innovations, in order to refine and polish the traditional techniques and practices of their own styles of business. An analysis of these techniques and practices, based on a wide range of actual case studies, would be invaluable for anyone seeking to improve their business practices. The efficacy and practicality of any management technique is put to the test only when transplanted from the soil in which it was nurtured to a new and different environment.

There is a great deal to be learned from such a study by both Japanese and foreign professionals. In this sense, the management techniques and legal practices newly adopted by Japan, and the Japanese management techniques and legal practices adopted by foreign countries, are an area of research that fully deserves the attention of scholars and experts both in Japan and abroad. These studies should serve as valuable test cases for the theory and practice of modern business. It is hoped that this casebook will be used as a starting point for such studies.

Reflecting this problem consciousness, my endeavor of case writing for Japanese companies and industries as teaching material has been very successful. Currently, 23 of my cases are listed online on Harvard Business Publishing (HBS) (https://hbsp.harvard.edu/home/) for sale in the US and the world, on the Asian Case Research Center (ACRC), University of Hong Kong (http://www.acrc.org.hk/) for sale in Asia, and on ECCH (the European Case Clearing House) (http://www.ecch.com/)

for sale in Europe. For my cases listed on HBS, visit https://hbsp.harvard.edu/search?N=&Nrpp=10&Ntt=MITSURU+MISAWA.

And see Figure 1A as follows for the list of the 23 cases on Harvard Business Online. Through Harvard, the total number of my cases sold in the past 15 years is **46,924** copies to worldwide universities and companies (for details, see Table 1A).

Top business schools of the world such as Harvard, MIT, and Wharton are constantly using my cases. Taking this opportunity, I decided to publish my second casebook containing my most recent seven cases for better serving the needs of the worldwide users of my case studies.

For the list of all the big users' names in 2021, see Table 2A. Top five big users are University of Hong Kong (Hong Kong), Indian Institute of Management (India), Monash University (Australia), International College of Management, Sydney (Australia), and IE Business School (Spain).

I would like to show the list of Largest Users of Misawa Cases over the past 15 years (2009–2021) in Table 3A. Among the constant big users, you will find notable names such as Harvard, University of Washington, MIT, Northwestern, USC, Wharton, NYU, and Cornell in the US, and University of Hong Kong (Hong Kong), SDA Bacconi School of Management (Italy), which is ranked 5th for MBA in Europe and 15th in the world by the *Financial Times*, and Instituto De Empresa, Business (Spain), which is ranked 1st in Europe in European Business School Ranking by *Financial Times*.

My recent case on Toshiba is the best seller at Harvard (see Table 4A and Figure 2A). The case is titled "The Toshiba Accounting Scandal: How Corporate Governance Failed." Through Harvard, 1,483 copies of my Toshiba case study were sold in 2021. For Toshiba's case, 6,964 copies (2,032 + 2,075 + 1,374 + 1,483) were sold in the past 4 years (2018–2021). This case has been very popular for the last few years and ranked among the top 20 most popular cases at Harvard.

My cases are being more widely used in the world in recent times (see Table 5A). The top 10 countries which are using my cases are Hong Kong, Australia, USA, India, China, Spain, Japan, UK, Italy, and the United Arab Emirates.

For this casebook to be used as course text, teaching notes have been prepared to assist course instructors. Faculty members of recognized academic institutions may apply for access to the teaching notes at:

Harvard Business Online (https://hbsp.harvard.edu/home/);

Asian Case Research Center (ACRC) at the University of Hong Kong (http:/www.acrc.org.hk/); and European Case Clearing House (http:/www.ecch.com/).

Multiple copies of individual cases may be ordered at the same websites.

Finally, I would like to express my deep appreciation to my two daughters, Anne Megumi Misawa and Marie Lei Misawa, who have provided me with continued support and encouragement during the writing of this casebook.

Mitsuru Misawa
Honolulu, Hawaii
15 January 2023

Appendix at the end of this book shows the sales record of my cases through Harvard Business Publishing Online. It includes the following:

Table 1A: Sales Record of My Cases in the Past 15 Years
Table 2A: The Users of Misawa's Cases in 2021
Table 3A: Largest Users of Misawa's Cases in the Past 15 Years (2007–2021)
Table 4A: Sales Records of Misawa's Cases in 2021
Table 5A: Sales Record of Misawa's Cases by Country in 2021

Figure 1A: Misawa's 21 Cases Listed on Harvard Business Publishing Online
Figure 2A: Misawa's Toshiba Case, the Best Seller at Harvard

About the Author

 **Mitsuru Misawa** received his LLB from Tokyo University Law School in 1960, LLM from Harvard Law School in 1964, MBA from the University of Hawaii at Manoa as an East-West Center grantee in 1965, and Ph.D. from the University of Michigan (International Finance) in 1967.

He is the Professor of Finance (International Finance and International Banking) and the Director of the Center for Japanese Global Investment and Finance at the University of Hawaii at Manoa, which was established in 1997 under the sponsorship of the Council for Better Corporate Citizenship of Japanese Keidanren (Japanese Federation of Economic Organizations). His tenure of University of Hawaii was granted in June, 1998.

Since 1 April 1997, he has been serving as Management Advisor for OSG Corp. in Japan.

Before he joined the University of Hawaii in August 1996, Dr. Misawa had been with Industrial Bank of Japan (IBJ), the most prestigious investment bank in Japan (now Mizuho Financial Group) for 30 years. His career included assignments as an investment banker in New York and Tokyo, for 15 years each. During his career at IBJ, he served as the Executive Vice President, IBJ Trust Bank (NY), Deputy General Manager, Loan Department, IBJ (Tokyo) in charge of large-scale companies such as Nissan, Sony, Komatsu, etc., the General Manager,

International Headquarter, IBJ (Tokyo), the President, IBJ Leasing (NY), and as a member of the Board of Directors, IBJ Leasing (Tokyo). One of the financial arrangements he conducted as an investment banker at IBJ was the Nissan Motor's direct investment to manufacture trucks and cars in Smyrna, Tennessee, in 1983. For total financing of $400 million, he employed "global financial engineering" techniques. Since then, these techniques have been widely used by other Japanese investors in the US.

From 1989 to 1996, Dr. Misawa served as the US Counselor on the Keidanren's "Council for Better Corporate Citizenship." From 1993 to 1996, he served as a member of the Business School's Visiting Committee of the University of Michigan, which was composed of global business executives. Further, Dr. Misawa was appointed "Colonel of the State of Kentucky" in 1984 and "Arkansas Traveler" in 1985 by those states in recognition of his achievements in soliciting Japanese investments for these states.

His researches have been published in numerous academic and professional journals, including *Sloan Management Review*, *Financial Management*, *The Columbia Journal of World Business*, *Vanderbilt Journal of Transnational Law*, *The Banking Law Journal*, *Temple International and Comparative Law Journal*, *Columbia Journal of Asian Law*, *Journal of International Law and Business* of Northwestern University School of Law, and *Penn State International Law Review* (The Dickinson School of Law).

His 23 Cases are listed in the US on Harvard Business Online. See Harvard Business Online under Misawa: https://hbsp.harvard.edu/search?N=&Nrpp=10&Ntt=MITSURU+MISAWA.

They are also listed on the European Case Clearing House (http://www.ecch.com/) in Europe and on the Asian Case Research Center (ACRC) at the University of Hong Kong (http:/www.acrc.org.hk/) in Asia.

Through them, he sold 2,060 copies of his cases in 2007, 1,555 copies in 2008, 1,895 copies in 2009, 2,327 copies in 2010, 1,492 copies in 2011, 1,798 copies in 2012, 2,575 copies in 2013, 2,778 copies in 2014, 4,085 copies in 2015, 2,833 copies in 2016, 4,093 copies in 2017, 5,158 copies in 2018, 4,607 copies in 2019, 4,630 copies in 2020, and 5,214 copies in 2021 (total number sold in the past 15 years is **46,924** copies) to worldwide universities and companies. Harvard Business School (MBA) purchased 1,063 copies of his cases for its own use in 2010. Other major universities such as MIT, USC, Wharton, and Cornell are also constant users of his cases.

Noteworthy in 2018 was that one of his recent cases on Toshiba was the best seller on Harvard. The case is titled "The Toshiba Accounting Scandal: How Corporate Governance Failed." Through Harvard, he sold 2,032 copies of Toshiba case in 2018, 2,075 copies in 2019, 1,374 copies in 2020, and 1,483 copies in 2021. The Toshiba case was very popular and ranked as the top 20 most popular cases at Harvard.

Besides these, Dr. Misawa published two books in the past:

In 2011, he published a book titled, *Current Business and Legal Issues in Japan's Banking and Finance Industry*, 2nd edition (5 chapters are added) (ISBN: 978-981-4291-01-9, 596 p.). World Scientific Publishing Co. Pte. Ltd., Singapore.

In 2016, Dr. Misawa published a book titled, *Cases on International Business and Finance in Japanese Corporations*, 2nd edition (ISBN: 978-981-4663-09-0, 546 p.). World Scientific Publishing Co. Pte. Ltd., Singapore.

For World Scientific Publishing Co. Pte. Ltd., see https://www.world scientific.com/page/about/corporate-profile.

"World Scientific publishes about 600 new titles a year and 160 journals in various fields. World Scientific has published more than 12,000 titles. Many of its books are recommended texts adopted by renowned institutions such as Harvard University, California Institute of Technology, Stanford University, and Princeton University."

"World Scientific broke new ground in 1991 when it signed a memorandum of agreement with the Nobel Foundation to publish the entire series of Nobel Lectures in all subjects — physics and astronomy, chemistry, physiology or medicine, economic sciences, and literature."

"In 1995, World Scientific co-founded the London-based Imperial College Press with London University's Imperial College. In 2006, the Press became a wholly owned subsidiary of World Scientific."

Dr. Misawa awards UH Professor Misawa–Honjo International Fellowship. A total fellowship amount of $30,000 has been granted to four to six recipients a year. The year of 2023 is the 16th year of this fellowship, and the total amount awarded to date is **$480,000**, with **67** students having received this fellowship so far. The funds are provided by Honjo International Scholarship Foundation. (See the web: https://www.hisf.or.jp/en/.)

The student can select any university in Japan such as Tokyo, Hitotsubashi, Keio, Waseda, Sophia, and ICU. The credits that UH students earn at Japanese universities are transferred toward their degrees at UH. They apply for Japanese universities through the exchange program at UH (MIX).

Acknowledgments

I am grateful to the following people who helped me publish this casebook.

First of all, I wish to thank the Asia Case Research Centre (ACRC), the University of Hong Kong, which has copyright for all my new seven cases in this book and who allowed publishing this casebook by World Scientific. It is a tremendous benefit for students to be able to purchase one book containing all of my new seven cases, rather than having to buy each case individually.

Also, I wish to thank Harvard Business Online, which has been listing all my 23 cases, including the new seven cases in this book. You can see my 23 cases through its website: https://hbsp.harvard.edu/search?N=&Nr pp=10&Ntt=MITSURU+MISAWA.

Through Harvard, the total number of my cases sold in the past 15 years is **46,924** copies to worldwide universities and companies.

(1) Harvard Business School (MBA) purchased 1,063 copies of my cases for its own use in 2010. Other major universities such as MIT, USC, Wharton, and Cornell are also constant users of my cases.
(2) Noteworthy was that one of my recent cases on Toshiba was the best seller on Harvard in 2018. The case is titled "The Toshiba Accounting Scandal: How Corporate Governance Failed." And this case is included in this book.

In my research for my cases, I had to visit Japanese companies, arrange interviews, and obtain reference materials. I am therefore indebted to the executives of these Japanese companies for their kind understanding and cooperation.

It was necessary for me to make several trips to Japan to complete my work. This would not have been possible without the research fund provided by Shidler College of Business, the University of Hawaii at Manoa. I wish to sincerely thank all these sources of help.

Above all, I wish to express my love and gratitude to my family, especially my two daughters, Anne Megumi Misawa and Marie Lei Misawa, for their support of this book and their contribution to my research.

My hometown is in Ina City, Nagano, Japan, an area known as Ina Valley for its beautiful mountains and rivers. My parents rest there. The University of Hawaii at Manoa, where my office is located, is in Blue Hawaii, an island paradise full of beautiful hibiscus flowers in the southern Pacific. When I worked on this casebook, I thought of my hometown thousands of miles away, and also admired the gentle undulation of beautiful Diamond Head through the window of my office.

Contents

Introduction

Case 1. Sales Tax Increase in 2014 Under Abenomics: The Japanese Government's Dilemma

On 1 October 2013, at a meeting of ruling party officials, Japanese Prime Minister Shinzo Abe said that he had decided to go ahead with a plan to increase the sales tax from 5% to 8%, beginning 1 April 2014. This tax hike had become law in August 2012, under the then-Prime Minister Yoshihiko Noda. Abe, faced with a choice he did not ask for, sought to make a decision he could live with. Deciding whether to raise the tax had proven very hard for him. He had to take extraordinary care weighing conditions. The Bank of Japan (BOJ) had already fired the first "arrow" of Abenomics, unconventional easing of the money supply. The second, fiscal stimulus was constrained by Japan's fiscal rebalancing goals. With regards to the third arrow, a strategy for economic growth, the government was still working out how to break entrenched regulations in farming and employment. Until the very last moment, Abe had to consider whether a tax increase would lead Japan back into the deep valley of deflation and economic stagnation.

Case 2. The Toshiba Accounting Scandal: How Corporate Governance Failed

This case presents a comprehensive overview of the Toshiba accounting scandal. It examines how the accounting irregularities in evidence at

Toshiba spread from a relatively minor case of accounting misrepresentation to corporate-wide deception ingrained in the cultural fabric of the organization. The research highlights how issues of corporate culture can undermine even the most robust corporate governance strategies, and examines some of the challenges Toshiba faces in its attempts to recover from the biggest accounting scandal in contemporary Japanese history.

In 2015, Toshiba, a conglomerate best known throughout the world for its electronics products, announced to the world that it has overstated profits by ¥151.8 billion (US$1.2 billion) over a seven-year period. The conduct of Toshiba's management and employees left a deep stain on Japan that threw corporate culture and corporate governance practices into turmoil. Although there were systems in place in Toshiba that had been specifically designed to prevent fraud, these procedures failed to function as they should have. In addition, the external auditing body that had been contracted to keep Toshiba on the straight and narrow had fundamentally failed in its duties. Corporate governance procedures were also highly dependent on Toshiba's top management and the development of a culture that fostered and supported honest reporting, as opposed to the rogue culture that had emerged.

Following the announcement of the reporting errors, Toshiba was set on a path to execute organizational changes that created a new corporate culture from the top down, by first instilling transparency and disclosure as core values. The Toshiba case highlights how a corporate governance system can work when it is supported by a corporate culture of honesty and transparency.

Through introducing managers of world corporations to the theories and concepts related to fair accounting and cultural values, this case study poses useful questions that highlight the actions executives need to take to ensure corporate governance systems are working effectively in order to avoid scandals like Toshiba's from emerging in their respective organizations.

There are significant differences between the management philosophy and techniques of Japanese companies and those employed in the US. These include both decision-making styles and the techniques of corporate governance. This case analyzes the corporate cultures, customs, and systems that are unique to Japanese corporations, as a means of presenting a comprehensive overview of how Japanese corporations function. By studying this Japanese case, executives will develop insights into the critical thinking skills they can employ to make strategic business decisions in their organizations.

Case 3. Interest-Rate Swap Offered by Sumitomo Mitsui Bank: Was This for Hedging or Speculation?

Sumitomo Mitsui Banking Corporation (the Bank) was found not to have breached its duty of explanation when an interest rate swap agreement had been executed between the Bank and a customer (the Company), under which fixed and floating interest rates would be swapped and the resulting difference settled.

The Company had borrowed substantially at floating interest rate and wanted to hedge against the risk associated with rising interest rates. The agreement set:

(1) ¥300 million as a notional principal.
(2) The fixed and floating interest rate payments would be swapped. The terms of payment by the Company to the Bank for the fixed interest rate were 2.445% p.a., and terms of payment by the Bank to the Company for the floating interest rate were three-month TIBOR + 0%.
(3) Payments would be made on the eighth day of the third month following 8 June 2005, and every third month thereafter during the transaction period from 8 March 2005 to 8 March 2011.

During the period from 8 June 2005 to 7 June 2006, the Company paid ¥8.8 million in total to the Bank as the difference between the fixed interest rate and the floating interest rate, and penalty interest payments due to delay. These payments were subject to the agreement in question.

The Company then sued the Bank and asserted that it had breached its duty of explanation, abused its superior bargaining position, and inappropriately and unfairly solicited this agreement with the Bank. The Company had a basic question as to whether this swap was for hedging or speculation, and claimed that the Bank had not fully explained the product and the risk involved.

The court's decisions in the case were made without any solid economic analysis. Although such analysis should have played a more prominent role in the process by which the court made a decision, it was not included in the sentencing and was therefore not available for public analysis. The author has prepared such an economic analysis for this case study, so that it can be employed to assess the court decision.

Case 4. Toyota's New Business Model: Creating a Sustainable Future

Many companies study the management strategies of other companies, adapting and learning from the experiences of large multinationals. But global corporations also need strategies that are capable of adapting to changing markets and profitability. Is it possible for these corporations to develop new and powerful insights from following the strategies of smaller firms?

The Toyota Motor Corporation's philosophy and business strategy is known as the "The Toyota Way" and it is globally recognized as an industry leader. Its managerial values and business methods are regarded as benchmark practices, guiding the processes and strategies of organizations worldwide, e.g., Toyota's Kanban method of inventory control, which facilitates just-in-time manufacturing, is seen as the optimal approach to inventory control.

Founded in Japan in 1937, the company grew rapidly. But a series of issues, resulting in a drop in vehicle sales and profitability, left Toyota's president, Akio Toyoda, considering how the company could find more sustainable growth and incorporate this new philosophy into its existing business model.

Toyoda is now a strong advocate for an alternative philosophy known as the *Nenrin* or "tree ring" strategy. He credits a small company, Ina Food, which makes agar, a traditional ingredient in Japanese food, as the source of Toyota's ongoing success.

Finding inspiration in Ina Food's 55 years of sustainable growth and profit, Toyoda now follows many of its key initiatives, and the corporate giant has become one of the largest corporations globally, while still promoting the virtues of slow and steady growth on an ongoing basis.

Case 5. Negative Interest Rates: The Bank of Japan Experience

After 20 years of deflation and weak growth in Japan, and even after the introduction of Abenomics, it seemed there was no way of stimulating the nation's economy. Could an unconventional monetary policy work?

Despite Prime Minister Shinzo Abe's new economic strategy, known as "Abenomics," being enacted in 2012, Japan's deflationary spiral continued. In an effort to stimulate economic growth, early in 2013 the BOJ stepped in, using quantitative and qualitative monetary easing (QQE) with the aim of achieving an inflation target of 2% in two years. At that time, the short-term prime interest rate was 1.475% per year.

By purchasing Japanese government bonds (JGBs), the BOJ's initial round of quantitative easing doubled its balance sheet to ¥130 trillion (US$1.1 trillion). But by 2014, with inflation stagnating below 1%, the central bank was forced to progress to a second, open-ended phase of QQE that committed to annual asset purchases of ¥80 trillion (US$678 billion), a strategy it planned to continue until the 2% target inflation rate was achieved.

Despite all efforts, Japan's economy remained weak. On 20 January 2016, the BOJ's governor, Haruhiko Kuroda, held a policy meeting in Tokyo, where the decision was made to introduce QQE with a negative interest rate.

Kuroda was aiming to deliver a 2% price stability target in the shortest possible time, with the bank regulating monetary easing by controlling three economic dimensions: interest rates, quantitative monetary policy, and qualitative monetary policy.

Quantitative monetary easing is used to stimulate an economy, making it easier for businesses to borrow money. To do this, the BOJ purchases large amounts of short-term government securities from the market in order to increase the money supply to the markets, thereby encouraging bank lending and business investment. It is regarded as an unconventional monetary policy.

It is termed unconventional because, by Japanese law, the BOJ isn't allowed to purchase newly issued short-term government securities, as this is defined as "self-financing." If this were allowed to occur, the government could get money at any time, for any amount. The BOJ's purchase of short-term government securities is legal only when it is done in a limited amount under extreme circumstances. It is regarded as an unconventional monetary policy if it is undertaken in order to increase the money supply to the markets.

In addition to quantitative monetary easing, the BOJ also bought government bonds with longer maturation dates, averaging between 7 and

12 years, and riskier securities like exchange-traded funds (ETFs) and Japanese real estate investment trusts (J-REITs) from the markets in order to further increase the money supply to the markets. These securities were qualitatively different from short-term JGBs. This new monetary policy is known as qualitative easing.

As the BOJ controls Japan's money supply, the conventional strategy to achieve its inflation target would have been to buy and sell government debt, as short-term JGBs, in small amounts. But in an unconventional move, the bank was buying these in large amounts. The central bank believed it needed both quantitative and qualitative monetary policies working together for monetary easing to attain an inflation target of 2%.

Central banks like the BOJ only use negative interest rates when the economy is stagnating and they have run out of other options. Negative rates are generally considered as encouraging irresponsible lending, fueling bubbles, and creating conditions likely to cause a financial crash. But this strategic move appears to be the only option left for Japan's central bank.

When QQE with a negative interest rate was introduced, the outstanding balance of JGBs held by the BOJ was ¥400 trillion, equivalent to 40% of the total outstanding JGBs issued. In April 2013, when the BOJ adopted QQE, the outstanding balance was ¥130 trillion — a threefold change in less than three years.

This case is ideally suited to students with a background in investment. The author uses this case for teaching both undergraduate and MBA students.

More specifically, the case has been used as part of the following courses: International finance for year-three undergraduate students (F321); Japanese Finance for Undergraduates (F490); and an MBA with International Finance (F610). It may also be used by students studying international business, international economics, and global finance.

International business major students may find the case useful in helping them to better understand the world's third-largest economy and how the Japanese way of doing business differs from others. It will also help them in gaining a greater understanding of the nation's business culture and policies — an area that is frequently misunderstood when dealing with Japanese companies.

Case 6. Rethinking Saizeriya's Currency Hedging Strategy

The success of popular Italian fast-food chain Saizeriya with Japanese consumers led to the company's public listing in Tokyo and a significant expansion into new markets in Asia, where its affordable restaurant menus included pizzas, pasta, and seafood, as well as rice dishes. Many of the ingredients included in its meals were sourced from Australian suppliers. The company had grown to around 1,500 businesses, which operated as subsidiaries, branches, and franchises, and the company planned for further growth.

The company's long-standing president, Issei Horino, was appointed to the position of representative director on Saizeriya's board in 2000. The silver-haired, 63-year-old corporate veteran became the multinational company's president in 2009, taking over the role from its founder, Yasuhiko Shogaki, who established the company in 1973. Although he relinquished his position as company president in 2009, Shogaki continued to be involved in Saizeriya's operations, as chairman of its board.

Faced with economic uncertainty that looked likely to continue, Issei Horino felt he needed to strengthen and create greater stability for the company as its share price in Japan, together with its profitability, had fallen. He was particularly concerned about costs associated with payments to the firm's Australian suppliers, since these were paid in Australian dollars.

Horino wondered if Saizeriya could use currency hedging to avoid financial losses and manage costs caused by unexpected fluctuations in exchange rates. He knew that Shogaki had previously used this method, and that the former president's decision resulted in near financial disaster for the company, in addition to costly court cases. Horino wondered if, by careful examination of all the steps the company took with its previous foreign currency coupon swaps, he could avoid the same mistakes and effectively use currency hedging as a tool to better manage the company's risks associated with the depreciation of the Japanese yen (JPY).

Case 7. Bank of Japan's Dilemma: Should Its Ultra-easy Monetary Policy End Under Inflationary Pressure and a Weak JPY?

As the threat of a wider monetary policy difference between Japan and the United States grew, the JPY fell swiftly against the US dollar (USD).

Although the BOJ maintained its aggressive monetary easing strategy, the US Federal Reserve began tightening its own monetary policy to combat growing inflation. A weak JPY benefits Japan's exporters because it increases their profits when repatriating money. But rising crude oil and other commodity prices are causes of concern because Japan is a resource-scarce country, so a weakening JPY increases import costs and slows household spending.

Does the BOJ need to reconsider its aggressive monetary easing? The central bank's ultra-loose monetary strategy includes massive purchases of risky assets and long-term government bonds (JGB) as it attempts to hold inflation at 2%. However, the government's increased spending to take advantage of historically low interest rates has weakened fiscal discipline.

To re-energize the economy, the BOJ needs to avoid exceeding its inflation target and any negative consequences because a rapid depreciation of the JPY would cause import prices to skyrocket and increase ordinary citizens' cost of living. The bank's actions need to be flexible, and it must be diligent in its purchases of government bonds to preclude that action from being misinterpreted as an attempt to repair Japan's massive budget shortfall.

The US Federal Reserve turned to quantitative easing after the financial crisis in 2008, and by November 2021 it started to look for a way out, with quantitative easing ending in March 2022. Meanwhile, the BOJ is starting to battle against deflation. Given how high the markets' expectations have risen, they could easily take a downturn if the BOJ fails to produce results. To sustain momentum, the bank also needs to maintain a dialogue with the markets. Adding to market concerns is the fact that Haruhiko Kuroda's tenure as the BOJ's Governor expires in April 2023.

Case 1

Sales Tax Increase in 2014 Under Abenomics: The Japanese Government's Dilemma[*]

On 1 October 2013, at a meeting of ruling party officials, Japanese Prime Minister Shinzo Abe said that he had decided to go ahead with a plan to increase the sales tax from 5% to 8%, beginning 1 April 2014.[1] Abe, faced with a choice he had not asked for, sought to make a decision he could live with (see Exhibit 1). This tax hike had become law in August 2012 under then-Prime Minister Yoshihiko Noda.

Japan's sales tax had a long and tortured political history. First proposed seriously in 1979, under then-Prime Minister Masayoshi Ohira, the idea was shelved under a hale of condemnation from ruling and opposition parties alike. It took a decade to come to fruition, and started at a modest 3%. In 1997, the government of Prime Minister Ryutaro

---

[*]Professor Mitsuru Misawa prepared this case for class discussion. Dr. Misawa is a professor of finance and director of the Center for Japanese Global Investment and Finance at the University of Hawaii at Manoa. This case is not intended to show effective or ineffective handling of decision or business processes. The authors might have disguised certain information to protect confidentiality. Cases are written in the past tense, this is not meant to imply that all practices, organizations, people, places, or facts mentioned in the case no longer occur, exist, or apply.
[1]Prime Minister of Japan and His Cabinet (1 October 2013). "Sales Tax Increase to 8%," http://www.kantei.go.jp/jp/96_abe/statement/2013/1001kaiken.html, accessed 17 June 2015.

Exhibit 1:   List of Selected Countries by Sales Tax Rate in 2014 (%)

	Last	Previous	Highest	Lowest
Argentina	21.00	21.00	21.00	21.00
Australia	10.00	10.00	10.00	10.00
Belgium	21.00	21.00	21.00	21.00
Brazil	19.00	19.00	19.00	19.00
Canada	5.00	5.00	7.00	5.00
China	17.00	17.00	17.00	17.00
Denmark	25.00	25.00	25.00	25.00
Euro Area	20.67	20.59	20.67	13.50
France	20.00	19.60	20.00	19.60
Germany	19.00	19.00	19.00	16.00
Greece	23.00	23.00	23.00	18.00
India	12.36	12.36	12.50	12.36
Italy	22.00	22.00	22.00	20.00
Japan	8.00	5.00	8.00	5.00
Malaysia	6.00	6.00	10.00	6.00
Mexico	16.00	16.00	16.00	15.00
Norway	25.00	25.00	25.00	25.00
Pakistan	17.00	16.00	17.00	15.00
Portugal	23.00	23.00	23.00	17.00
Russia	18.00	18.00	18.00	18.00
Singapore	7.00	7.00	7.00	5.00
South Korea	10.00	10.00	10.00	10.00
Spain	21.00	21.00	21.00	16.00
Sweden	25.00	25.00	25.00	25.00
Switzerland	8.00	8.00	8.00	7.60
Taiwan	5.00	5.00	5.00	5.00
Thailand	7.00	7.00	7.00	7.00
United Kingdom	20.00	20.00	20.00	8.00
United States	0.00	0.00	0.00	0.00

Source: Trading Economics, "List of Selected Countries by Sales Tax Rate," http://www.tradingeconomics.com/country-list/sales-tax-rate, accessed 30 July 2014.

Hashimoto fell after giving the go-ahead for a hike to 5%, which had the ill luck of coinciding with the Asian financial crisis.

Abe said raising the sales tax from 5% to 8% on 1 April 2014, was necessary to make the social security system sustainable and maintain confidence in the Japanese government's finances.[2] Abe thought that the sales tax hike was the best scenario for the economy and that it would not hamper Japan's economic growth. He expressed confidence that the government could ease any potential negative economic impact of the higher sales tax by employing various stimulus measures.[3] His position was that the government urgently needed to secure revenue to finance the state budget, which had been increasingly under pressure from swelling welfare costs, and therefore the sales tax rate had to be increased as scheduled.[4] Abe vowed to take steps to prevent the sales tax hike from undermining Japan's nascent economic recovery, stressing that the government could achieve a balance between economic growth and fiscal discipline.[5]

Sales Tax Increase Pluses and Minuses

It was imperative that the government give a full account of economic and fiscal conditions, tax revenues, and stimulus measures. A rise of one point in the sales tax rate brought JPY2.7tn[6] in additional revenue to Japan. Thus, raising the tax from 5% to 8% in April 2014 should have generated an extra JPY8.1tn in revenue per year, beginning in fiscal 2014.[7] It then seemed reasonable for the Japanese government to introduce a fairly large package of stimulus measures with this newly generated revenue.

After Abe officially announced, on 1 October 2013, the decision to raise the sales tax, Japanese industries like auto plants began increasing production to meet an expected surge in demand before the tax hike took effect. Automakers were raising production by increasing work hours rather than expanding their physical plants, because demand was seen as certain to weaken after the tax hike.

Abe believed that expanding private-sector investment was absolutely critical. Japanese companies were sitting on a JPY220tn cash reserve.

---

[2] *Ibid.*

[3] *Ibid.*

[4] Prime Minister of Japan and His Cabinet (1 October 2013). "Large-Scale Tax Cuts to Counter Sales Tax Hike," http://www.kantei.go.jp/jp/96_abe/statement/2013/1001kaiken. html, accessed 17 June 2015.

[5] *Ibid.*

[6] USD26.21bn at the rate of JPY103.03/USD on 1 April 2014.

[7] *Ibid.*

If the Japanese government were to achieve its goal of sustained economic growth, it needed to help companies use that cash reserve effectively by creating an environment favorable to business, especially as Japanese companies must have developed new markets inside and outside the country. To lessen the slowdown, the Japanese government considered offering corporate income tax breaks to encourage companies to increase pay and capital spending (see Exhibit 1). Japan's corporate income tax, which was 35.64% in 2014, was very high by international standards. Beginning in April 2015, Japan would reduce it by about 2½%, as part of Abe's push to resuscitate his growth-revival plan.[8] Cutting the country's corporate taxes was necessary to enhance the competitiveness of Japanese companies and make Japan a more attractive destination for foreign investment.

For Japanese industries to take advantage of corporate income tax breaks and deregulation, they needed to shake up their managements, create added value, and deal with the challenge of globalization. Construction-machinery maker Komatsu plowed part of the profits it earned overseas back into R&D and employment in Japan. Komatsu believed that it could increase work in Japan when it expanded operations overseas.[9]

Manufacturers such as automakers were faced with the reality that emerging economies accounted for 90% of global market growth. Japanese automakers found it difficult to invest at home, since they had surplus auto-making capacity in Japan. The new assembly plants and expanded factories announced by Mazda Motor Corp and Honda Motor Co. Ltd. in 2014 were not in Japan, but more than 2,000 miles away, in Thailand. Toyota said that it could barely maintain employment, much less think about raising wages.[10] Over the past three decades, the automobile, electrical equipment, and materials industries had underpinned capital spending in Japan, but in recent years, that role had been taken over increasingly by telecommunications, health care, and other services.

With respect to corporate capital spending, for example, the Japanese market for self-driving vehicles was expected to grow to around JPY10tn in the future, giving a lift to satellite communications, artificial

---

[8] *Wall Street Journal* (30 December 2014). "Japan to Lower Corporate Tax Rate," http://www.wsj.com/articles/japan-to-lower-corporate-tax-rate-1419935308, accessed 20 April 2014.

[9] Komatsu, Annual Report (2013). https://www.komatsu.jp/en/ir/library/annual, accessed 20 April 2014.

[10] *Ibid.*

intelligence, and other technologies.[11] Although the competition to put such vehicles to practical use was heating up worldwide, they were barred from public roads in Japan. If the automakers could persuade the Japanese government to relax these rules, they would gain valuable experience while enhancing Japan's transportation capacity. Japanese automakers were calling for the creation of a special zone near the venues of the 2020 Summer Olympics in Tokyo, where self-driving cars would be allowed to operate freely. This was an effort Japanese industry needed to "manufacture the future." It was important to establish a virtuous growth cycle beginning in Japan, running through the rest of the world, and returning to Japan.

"Bumpy" Road Ahead for Abe

Abe considered the road ahead could be "somewhat bumpy." After taking the plunge on raising the sales tax, Abe would face challenges to solidifying the gains of Abenomics. The Abe government decided to compile a new economic stimulus package worth about JPY5tn to cushion the blow of the consumption tax hike from 5% to 8%.[12] Keynesians preferred government spending over private spending, and Abe wanted to place priority on government spending, which would boost the economy more quickly. But government spending was financially constrained. He also believed tax cuts for businesses would have a big economic impact.[13] Actually, he was more concerned about fostering a virtuous cycle in which stronger corporate earnings led to wage increases. Abe believed that if people did not see the benefits of his economic policies in the form of higher pay, Abenomics[14] would be a failure.[15]

---

[11] *Ibid.*

[12] Prime Minister of Japan and His Cabinet (10 October 2013). "Bumpy Road Ahead for Abenomics," http://www.kantei.go.jp/jp/96_abe/statement/2013/1010naigai.html, accessed 17 June 2015.

[13] *Ibid.*

[14] "Abenomics" were the economic policies advocated by Japanese Prime Minister Shinzo Abe in 2013. There were three components of Abenomics: monetary easing, fiscal spending, and growth strategies. For the details of Abenomics, see Misawa, M. (2013). *Abenomics of Japan: What Was It? Could This Conquer Japan's Decade-Long Deflation?* 13/534C, Asian Case Research Center (ACRC), The University of Hong Kong.

[15] *Ibid.*

The government had pressed Japanese companies to do their part by boosting wages and capital spending. Stimulating growth in exchange for lower corporate taxes, Abe instructed the Ministry of Finance (MOF) to consider multiple options for raising the sales tax, including an adjustment of the increase's size and the timing.[16] He believed that the tug-of-war within the government over possible changes to the tax increase was just a sideshow aimed at putting pressure on the MOF to agree to a large economic stimulus package. The government's approach to stimulating the corporate sector, which promised favorable policy measures in exchange for companies' cooperation on various issues, offered the benefits of lower taxes (see Exhibit 2).

The Abe government's eagerness to achieve a quick economic recovery by putting pressure on businesses had led to general apprehension:

(1)   The government would be watching closely, and could be expected to praise businesses that raised wages and criticize those that did not. Japanese workers were getting a push from Abe's call for pay hikes, but worries over the global economic outlook could make companies think twice about paying workers more. It gave the government a larger say in plans and decisions traditionally left in private hands. For example, the Federation of All Toyota Workers' Unions,[17] an umbrella group for labor unions at more than 300 Toyota Motor Corp. group companies, was split into two groups: One saw Abe's call as the first good opportunity for wage hikes in five years. The other group was looking for lump-sum pay-outs, because it believed the auto industry could no longer afford continuous pay increases.[18] Some business leaders complained the government would use tax breaks as a way to monitor companies' inner workings more closely and pressure them to raise worker pay.[19] Some other business leaders were unhappy about being asked to provide the government with data on individual

---

[16] *Ibid.*

[17] For details on this union, see Toyota Global Website (2014) "75 Years of TOYOTA," TOYOTA MOTOR CORPORATION GLOBAL WEBSITE, 75 Years of TOYOTA, Labor-Management Relations, Outline (toyota-global.com), accessed 20 April 2014.

[18] IMF, "Abenomics — Time for a Push from Higher Wages", https://www.imf.org/en/Blogs/Articles/2014/03/20/abenomics-time-for-a-push-from-higher-wages, accessed 20 April 2014.

[19] *Ibid.*

Exhibit 2:   Corporate Tax Rates for Selected Countries (%)

Years	Australia	Brazil	China	France	Germany	Hong Kong	India	Japan	Mexico	Russia	Singapore	Taiwan	United Kingdom	United States
2006	30	34	33	33.33	38.34	17.5	33.66	40.69	29	24	20	25	30	40
2007	30	34	33	33.33	38.36	17.5	33.99	40.69	28	24	20	25	30	40
2008	30	34	25	33.33	29.51	16.5	33.99	40.69	28	24	18	25	30	40
2009	30	34	25	33.33	29.44	16.5	33.99	40.69	28	20	18	25	28	40
2010	30	34	25	33.33	29.41	16.5	33.99	40.69	30	20	17	17	28	40
2011	30	34	25	33.33	29.37	16.5	32.44	40.69	30	20	17	17	26	40
2012	30	34	25	33.33	29.48	16.5	32.45	38.01	30	20	17	17	24	40
2013	30	34	25	33.33	29.55	16.5	33.99	38.01	30	20	17	17	23	40
2014	30	34	25	33.33	29.58	16.5	33.99	35.64	30	20	17	17	21	40

Source: KPMG, "Corporate Tax Rate Survey 2014," https://www.kpmg.com/sg/en/issuesandinsights/articlespublications/pages/tax-tax-corporate-and-indirect-tax-rate-survey-2014.aspx.

companies' wage increases.[20] They said that the effect of tax breaks on companies' bottom lines was hard to measure, although it was possible to provide basic data.[21]

(2) As tax breaks stimulated capital spending, companies that invested in cutting-edge facilities would be allowed to choose between booking depreciation charges in one year or deducting 5% of the investment from their corporate tax bill. The Japanese government considered toughening regulations to make large-scale buildings and other facilities more quake-resistant and energy-efficient, in order to amplify the tax breaks' effects.[22] But, in return, industries would be collecting data on additional investment plans at individual companies. Some industries thought this was the government getting priorities wrong.[23] They thought the government neither could nor should leave Japan's economic rejuvenation in the hands of the corporate sector, while shelving its own midterm fiscal rehabilitation plan.[24]

To Tackle Welfare and Regulation

Abenomics could be deemed a success only if Abe's government was able to clear the major hurdle of curbing Japan's burgeoning social security costs. Abe's government had to rethink Japan's regulatory structure. The Japanese government spent about JPY30tn annually on social security programs, which was a major reason why government debt had grown to twice the size of Japan's GDP (see Exhibit 3). Japan's healthcare, nursing care, and pension benefits totaled more than JPY100tn annually, and the bill was rising due to the country's aging population. It was estimated that Japan would have to raise the sales tax to more than 30% if it intended to stabilize the government's finances on the basis of this measure alone.[25]

---

[20] This was the result of a survey by Nikkei Inc. and TV Tokyo Corp. in October 2013. For details, see: Nihon Keizai Shinbun (3 October 2013). "Abe's scandals deserve scrutiny," *The Japan Times*, http://e.nikkei.com/e/ac/tnks/Nni20131003D03HH121.htm, accessed 20 April 2014.

[21] *Ibid.*

[22] *Ibid.*

[23] *Ibid.*

[24] *Ibid.*

[25] Supra note 1.

Exhibit 3: Public Debt-to-GDP Ratio of the Selected Countries in 2014

Country	Percentage of GDP
Japan	227.70
Greece	174.50
Italy	134.10
Portugal	131.00
Ireland	118.90
Singapore	106.70
Belgium	101.90
Spain	97.60
France	95.50
Iceland	94.00
Egypt	93.80
Canada	92.60
United Kingdom	86.60
Germany	74.70
United States	71.20
Brazil	59.30
India	51.30
Thailand	48.60
Philippines	48.40
Mexico	41.00
South Korea	37.20
Hong Kong	37.00
Taiwan	36.50
Switzerland	34.70
Australia	34.50
China	22.40
Russia	13.40
Saudi Arabia	1.60

Source: US, CIA, World Fact Book, "Public Debt-to-GDP Ratio of the Selected Countries in 2014," https://www.cia.gov/the-world-factbook/, accessed 20 April 2015.

It was also estimated that the employee pension program would exhaust its reserves in 2038 if no changes were made to the system.[26] Abe's government was reluctant to rein in social security spending, although such cuts would be needed to avoid large tax hikes in the future.

To keep the system solvent, the government had to consider raising the eligibility age and taking a fresh look at the balance between contributions and benefits. Given the pension system's actual return on assets and the amount of unpaid premiums, the government was far from being able to promise security for 100 years, as it had once done.[27]

During former Prime Minister Junichiro Koizumi's term, from 2001 to 2006, the government moved to reduce the growth of social security spending by JPY220bn per year for five years, beginning in 2007. This decision led to the defeat of the Liberal Democratic Party in the subsequent election, as older voters deserted the government in droves. Pension benefits offered a prime example of how such considerations affect policy. Legislators tried to avoid antagonizing the elderly, who were politically powerful because they voted in greater numbers than the young.

Deregulation was crucial to Japan's long-term economic health. Done properly, it would raise Japan's potential growth rate by promoting competition and innovation. Abenomics was unlikely to succeed if the government rested on the laurels of its successful monetary policy, and shied away from difficult reforms needed to establish a sustainable welfare system and an effective growth strategy. As the first big test of Abe's appetite for reform, the government would conduct a review of medical fees when it drew up a budget for fiscal 2014 at the end of 2013. Another area yet to be tackled was reform aimed at changing "bedrock regulations" in medical and nursing care, agriculture, and employment. But Abe would need to show strong leadership to overcome resistance from government ministries and industries that benefited from the *status quo*.

Rating Agency's Position

At that time in the US, Moody's Investors Service gave Japanese long-term credit an Aa3, equivalent to AA-, and saw its outlook as stable.[28] It believed that the tax hike was necessary for Japan to control the issuance

---

[26] *Ibid.*

[27] *Ibid.*

[28] *Ibid.*

of government debts, which had reached very high levels,[29] and to maintain the credibility of Japanese government bonds among market players. It said in a report on 3 October 2013, that it gave the rating of "credit positive" to the Japanese government's decision to raise the sales tax rate beginning in April 2014.[30] The ratings agency also said in the report that the increased revenue to be brought in by the tax hike would contribute to rebuilding Japan's fiscal health.[31]

It pointed out further that stimulus measures would be necessary to ease the impact the tax hike would have on economic activity.[32] It said market players might demand high-risk premiums from Japanese bonds if losses reflected in balancing the Japanese budget were not reduced.[33] If this happened, costs for fund procurement and bond refinancing by the Japanese government would be high. Given all this, Abe said, on the same day, that the government would implement stimulus measures worth JPY5tn when the sales tax rate was raised from 5% to 8%.[34] However, Abe's growth strategy lacked specific measures for fiscal renovation, despite the growth strategy being one of the three key policy components of Abenomics.

Economic Outlook for 2014

Abe was allowed to conduct a "Review of the State of the Economy" before his decision to increase the sales tax from 3% to 5% on 1 April 2014. On 22 December 2013, just before the decision, the Japanese government forecast that the nominal GDP growth rate would grow by 1.4% in 2014.[35] The government's growth projection in real terms, together with

---

[29]The ratio of Japanese government debt to GDP averaged 121.76% from 1980 until 2014, reaching an all-time high of 230% in 2014. For details, see Trading Economics (2015). "Japan Government Debt to GDP," http://www.tradingeconomics.com/japan/government-debt-to-gdp, accessed 30 August 2015.

[30]*Ibid.*

[31]*Ibid.*

[32]*Ibid.*

[33]*Ibid.*

[34]*Ibid.*

[35]Prime Minister of Japan and His Cabinet (21 December 2013). "Economic Outlook for 2014," https://www.cao.go.jp/, accessed 10 September 2015.

See also Japanese Cabinet Office (20 April 2014). "Indexes of Business Conditions," http://www.esri.cao.go.jp/en/stat/di/die.htm.

Exhibit 4:   Japan GDP Growth Rate: 2012–2015

The Gross Domestic Product (GDP) in Japan expanded 0.40% in the fourth quarter of 2014 over the previous quarter. GDP Growth Rate in Japan averaged 0.49% from 1980 until 2014, reaching an all-time high of 3.20% in the second quarter of 1990 and a record low of –4% in the first quarter of 2009. GDP Growth Rate in Japan is reported by the Cabinet Office, Japan.

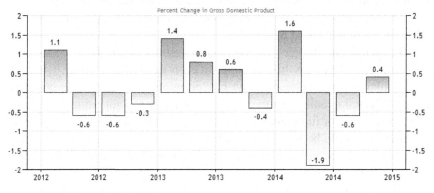

Source: Trading Economics, "Japan GDP Growth Rate: 2012–2015," http://www.tradingeconomics.com/japan/gdp-growth, accessed 30 July 2014.

2013's 2.6% growth, indicated that Japan's economy had continued to recover moderately on the strength of Abenomics, despite expected negative impact associated with the sales tax hike, which would stifle consumer spending by decreasing real household income (see Exhibit 4).[36]

The forecast consumer price index, excluding fresh food, was +1.2% above the previous year, the highest rate of increase since October 2008.[37] The government's price projection also signaled a possible end to nearly two decades of deflation, as a result of the BOJ's ultra-easy monetary policy, introduced in April 2013 (see Exhibit 5). With prices rising, the nominal GDP growth rate was set to expand to 3.3%, up from 2.5% in 2013.[38] The nominal GDP was projected to reach JPY500.4tn in 2014.[39] This would be the first time in seven years the nominal GDP topped

---

[36] *Ibid.*
[37] *Ibid.*
[38] *Ibid.*
[39] *Ibid.*

Exhibit 5:   Japan Consumer Price Index

CPI in Japan decreased to 102.90 Index Points in February of 2015 from 103.10 Index Points in January of 2015. CPI in Japan averaged 72.54 Index Points from 1957 until 2015, reaching an all time high of 104.50 Index Points in October of 1998 and a record low of 18 Index Points in February of 1957. CPI in Japan is reported by the Statistics Bureau, Japan.

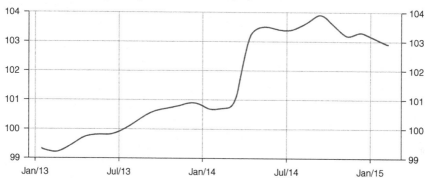

Notes: (1) 2010 = 100.

(2) In Japan, CPI measures changes in the prices paid by consumers for a basket of goods and services.

Source: Statistics Bureau, Japan, "Japan Consumer Price Index (CPI)," http://www.tradingeconomics. com/japan/consumer-price-index-cpi, accessed 20 April 2015.

JPY500tn, recovering to a level prior to the 2008 onset of the global financial crisis. If projections were realized, the nominal GDP growth rate would also surpass the real rate for the first time in 17 years.

Along with improved corporate profits, corporate capital investment would expand a real 4.4%.[40] As corporate performance continued to be favorable, corporate sector confidence was rising, and the drive to invest was strengthening. But in the wake of the sales tax hike, consumer spending was expected to grow only 0.45%, and housing investment was likely to fall 3.2%.[41]

The Japanese government anticipated the yen exchange rate would average JPY100 to the dollar in 2014 (see Exhibit 6).[42] Exports were projected to expand 5.4% due to the weaker yen, which worked in favor of

---

[40] *Ibid.*

[41] *Ibid.*

[42] *Ibid.*

Exhibit 6:   Yen/$: January 2010–May 2015

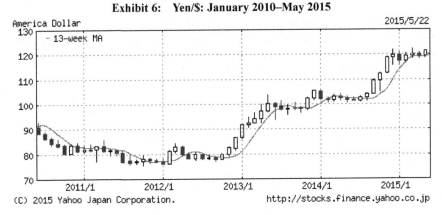

Source: Yahoo! Finance, "Yen/$," https://finance.yahoo.co.jp/, accessed 30 July 2014.

export-oriented manufacturing companies, improving their profitability.[43] At the same time, imports were forecast to increase 3.5%, which would mean Japan's trade balance would improve slightly from the previous year.[44] In 2013, Japan logged a record trade deficit due to sharp increases in import of fossil fuel for expanded thermal power generation, given the shutdown of Japan's nuclear power plants following the March 2011 accident at the Fukushima Daiichi Nuclear Power Station.

In Japan, labor shortages were becoming more serious. Japan's jobless rate was forecast to fall from 3.9% to 3.7% in 2014.[45] In an effort to cushion the potential negative economic impact of the sales tax hike, the Japanese government finalized an emergency economic stimulus package worth JPY5.5tn in December 2014, hoping to boost the nation's real GDP by as much as 0.7%.[46] In so doing, the Cabinet Office pledged to create at least 250,000 jobs.[47] Quantitative easing by the BOJ, which was expected to continue, should also have served to provide underlying support to the economy.

---

[43] *Ibid.*

[44] *Ibid.*

[45] *Ibid.*

[46] *Ibid.*

[47] *Ibid.*

The Decision Time for Abe

No matter which government creates a policy or when, the good or bad of it rests with the government at the time it is carried out.[48]

— Prime Minister Shinzo Abe

It was early October 2013, and this was the time for Abe to make his final decision to move ahead with a Diet-approved sales tax rise from 5% to 8% in April 2014. Deciding whether to raise the tax had proven very hard for him. He had to take extraordinary care weighing conditions.

The BOJ had already fired the first "arrow" of Abenomics, an unconventional easing of the money supply. The BOJ was aggressively buying large quantities of government bonds under this loose monetary policy. If this was misinterpreted as printing money to finance government debt, interest rates might surge. The second "arrow," fiscal stimulus, was constrained by Japan's fiscal rebalancing goals. Raising the sales tax should send a message to the markets that the Japanese government was resolved to pay the debt on its own. As for the third "arrow," a strategy for economic growth, the government was still working out how to break entrenched regulations in farming, employment, and other areas.

When the sales tax rate was raised from 3% to 5% in 1997, then-Prime Minister Ryutaro Hashimoto said, on 31 March 1997, the day before the increase, "This was a reform our generation must undertake for the sake of future generations."[49] But Hashimoto's Liberal Democratic Party lost big in the lower house election the following year, spelling the end of his government. This bitter experience made the sales tax a political third rail, and Abe had kept the option of delaying the tax hike open until the very last moment. He was especially concerned about dissatisfaction in the hinterlands, which had lagged behind cities in economic recovery. This could work against the tax increase in the next upper house election in 2016.

Until the very end, Abe thought through whether a tax increase would lead Japan back into the deep valley of deflation and economic stagnation. He had various questions before him, as follows:

---

[48] Supra note 1.
[49] *Ibid.*

(1) The nightmare scenario for Abe was that the Japanese economy would take a turn for the worse after the sales tax went up. An economic slowdown could sap his political momentum. Would it happen?

(2) Abe was seeking an elusive virtuous cycle of bigger corporate profits leading to higher wages and more jobs. What he did not want was for households to feel the pinch of a tax hike before partaking in an economic recovery. He believed Abenomics would not succeed unless it begot wage growth and promoted consumer spending. That would keep Japan mired in deflation. Would households feel the same way?

(3) Abe took charge of crafting his government's latest economic stimulus package, insisting on lowering the corporate tax rate to fight against deflation, rather than simply holding the line. Abe was aware of criticism that he was lavishing rewards on corporations, but he could argue that his policies would eventually lead to higher wages and more jobs. Would his policies work?

(4) Abe tended to favor economic growth over fiscal rebalancing, arguing the latter was impossible without the former. He believed that cutting the corporate tax would mean a temporary drop in tax revenue, which would then eventually increase as industry became more robust. Abe's position was that a growing economy and healthier public finances were not mutually exclusive goals. Would his position be workable?

(5) In early 2015, Abe would have to conduct a "Review of the State of the Economy," deciding whether to proceed with the next stage of the sales tax increase, from 8% to 10%, in October 2015. Would economic conditions in 2015 be good enough to support a decision to raise the sales tax to 10%?

Conclusion

If we raise taxes now, would consumption slump, and would the Japanese economy sink back into the deep valley that is economic morass and deflation? I pondered these questions until the very end. But there is no road left for us but to grow our economy and to rebuild our finances at the same time.

— Prime Minister Shinzo Abe[50]

[50] *Ibid.*

In a televised news conference on 1 October 2013, Abe said he would stick to a plan to raise the sales tax rate in April 2014 from 5% to 8%, in a bid to tackle Japan's enormous debt. This was the first increase in 17 years. In his public announcement the same day, he added the need to maintain confidence in Japan's fiscal health and pay for the country's growing number of elderly citizens. He assured that he would initiate a stimulus package of roughly JPY6tn so that this tax increase would not put the brakes on Japan's nascent economic recovery.[51]

He was confident in his decision. By that time, quantitative easing, the first "arrow" of Abenomics, had yielded positive results. It had changed market sentiment significantly and brought about the yen's depreciation and higher stock prices. The yen sharply decreased in value, crossing the JPY100/USD1 boundary. This yen depreciation promoted export profitability, which in turn led to rising stock prices. The Nikkei average had more than doubled since the Abenomics rally began in November 2012, outperforming the Dow Jones Industrial Average in the US, which rose 40% over the same period (see Exhibit 7).

However, the sales tax increase in April 2014 was set to be followed by a second increase in October 2015. This would take the rate to 10%, although the plan allowed the government to conduct a "Review of the State of the Economy" before raising the sales tax again.

Exhibit 7: 2 Years' Trend of Japanese Stocks: April 2013–April 2015

(C) 2015 Yahoo Japan Corporation.   http://stocks.finance.yahoo.co.jp

Source: Yahoo! Finance, "Trend of Japanese Stocks," https://finance.yahoo.co.jp/, accessed 30 July 2014.

---

[51] *Ibid.*

Deciding whether to raise the sales tax to 10% would prove even harder for the Abe administration. On 31 March 2015, it decided to postpone the scheduled increase to 10% from October 2015 to April 2017, in an attempt to boost economic activity.[52] Abe's administration was concerned that the sales tax hike had effected a sharp drop in personal consumption. This postponement of the sales tax hike heightened uncertainty over Japan's ability to achieve fiscal consolidation. The tax hike in April 2017 didn't have any escape clause; the government would not be allowed to conduct another "Review of the State of the Economy" beforehand. But the Abe administration's basic premise for the additional tax hike was there would be an end to deflation by that time.

For Further Discussion

(1) What were the expected economic effects of the sales tax increase on the Japanese economy?

(2) Until the last moment, Abe considered whether a tax increase would lead Japan back into the deflation and economic stagnation it had suffered for the last 20 years. Comment on the deflationary spiral Japan had suffered.

(3) On 1 October 2013, Japanese Prime Minister Shinzo Abe decided to go ahead with the plan to increase the sales tax from 5% to 8%, beginning 1 April 2014. To lessen economic slowdown, the Japanese government offered corporate income tax breaks to encourage companies to increase pay and capital spending. There was consumer criticism that Abe was lavishing rewards on corporations while sacrificing consumers. How would you defend Abe and his policies' tax fairness?

(4) Under Abenomics, it was said that the Japanese government and the Bank of Japan were very well coordinated. Comment on how monetary and fiscal policy coordination should be maintained.

(5) Foreign e-commerce firms in Japan were not paying sales tax. Why not? Was this a double standard?

(6) Do you believe markets welcomed Abe's official decision to increase the consumption tax to 8% in 2014?

---

[52]National Diet of Japan (31 March 2015). "Sales Tax 10% Is to Be Postponed to April, 2017," http://kokkai.ndl.go.jp/cgibin/KENSAKU/swk_dispdoc.cgi?SESSION=38914& SAVED_RID=2&PAGE=0&POS=0&TOTAL=0&SRV_ID=10&DOC_ID=3451&DPAGE= 16&DTOTAL=425&DPOS=315&SORT_DIR=1&SORT_TYPE=0&MODE=1& DMY=39333, accessed 17 June 2015.

Case 2

The Toshiba Accounting Scandal: How Corporate Governance Failed*

Toshiba Corporation expresses sincere apologies to our shareholders, customers, business partners and all other stakeholders for any concern or inconvenience caused by issues relating to the appropriateness of its accounting treatments. With the new management team and governance structure, Toshiba as a whole will unite to make every effort to regain the trust of shareholders, investors, all other stakeholders and members of the public, and asks for your understanding and ongoing support.

— Toshiba Corporation[1]

---

*Professor Mitsuru Misawa prepared this case for class discussion. Dr. Misawa is a professor of finance and director of the Center for Japanese Global Investment and Finance at the University of Hawaii at Manoa. This case is not intended to show effective or ineffective handling of decision or business processes. The authors might have disguised certain information to protect confidentiality. Cases are written in the past tense, this is not meant to imply that all practices, organizations, people, places or fact mentioned in the case no longer occur, exist or apply.

[1]Toshiba IR News (n.d.). "Home Page," http://www.toshiba.co.jp/about/ir/index.htm, accessed 1 August 2016.

Toshiba CEO Resigns amid Major Accounting Scandal

Toshiba Corporation (Toshiba) hit the headlines in 2015 for all the wrong reasons. Following an internal audit, it emerged that the accounts of the Japanese conglomerate, which manufactured everything from consumer electronics to nuclear energy technology, contained major irregularities, and that profits had been significantly inflated (see Exhibit 1). The scandal, which first came to light when Toshiba itself investigated the accounting practices of the group's energy division in April 2015,[2] led to the resignation of then-Chief Executive and President, Hisao Tanaka, in September of that year, along with eight additional board members, including Vice Chairman Norio Sasaki.[3] Stepping into the breach, Toshiba's new president and CEO, Masashi Muromachi,[4] immediately instructed a third-party committee to conduct a detailed audit of the group's accounting practices. The findings of this review revealed that Toshiba had overstated profits by JPY151.8bn (USD1.2bn) over a seven-year period.[5] When, in September 2015, the full and accurate financial results were finally released for the fiscal year ending 31 March 2015,[6] it emerged that the firm had suffered a cumulative net loss of more than JPY255.5bn (USD2.14bn) over the previous seven years.[7] All dividend

---

[2]*Ibid.*

[3]Nikkei (21 June 2015). "Toshiba's Accounting Scandal," http://www.nikkei.com/article/ DGXZZO89536830R20C15A7000000/, accessed 1 August 2016.

[4]Toshiba IR News (7 September 2015). "Notice of New Representative Executive Officers," http://www.toshiba.co.jp/about/ir/en/news/20150907_3.pdf, accessed 1 August 2016.

[5]Toshiba IR News (8 May 2015). "Notice Regarding Establishment of Independent Investigation Committee," http://www.toshiba.co.jp/worldwide/index.html, accessed 1 August 2016.

[6]Toshiba IR News (7 September 2015). "Notice on Restatement of Past Financial Results, Outline of FY2014 Consolidated Business Results, Submission of 176th Annual Securities Report and Outline of Recurrence Prevention Measures, etc.," http://www.toshiba.co.jp/about/ir/en/news/20150907_1.pdf, accessed 1 August 2016.

[7]Nikkei (7 September 2015). "Toshiba Reveals 230bn Yen in Losses in PCs, Appliances," http://asia.nikkei.com/Markets/Tokyo-Market/Toshiba-reveals-230bn-yen-in-losses-in-PCs-appliances, accessed 1 August 2016.

Exhibit 1:   Toshiba's Corporate Profile

Business Summary

Toshiba Corp. was founded in July 1875, and is headquartered in Tokyo, Japan. It employs around 200,000 employees. The company manufactures and sells electronic and electrical products in five principal domains, as follows:

- Energy & Infrastructure, which offers hydro, solar, geothermal, and wind power generation facilities in the renewable energy space, as well as thermal, hydroelectric, and nuclear power generation systems. The Energy & Infrastructure division also supplies power transmission and distribution systems that deliver electricity to homes, commercial facilities, and other users. It is also a source of social infrastructure solutions in fields ranging from transportation and security to automation and telecommunications.
- Community Solutions, which covers city infrastructure support management of energy, water, and other essentials across building, home, commerce, and retail solutions.
- Healthcare Systems & Services, which provides healthcare system and service solutions in four areas: Diagnostics & Treatment for early detection and stress-free, patient-friendly therapy; Prevention to reduce the risk of disease onset or ameliorate its impact; Prognosis & Nursing Care to support patients and their caregivers; and Health Promotion to contribute to mental and physical health and to the safety of food, water, and air.
- Electronic Devices & Components, which handles the development of NAND Flash memories, the semiconductor business, and the system LSI business.
- Lifestyle Products & Services, which includes digital products like LCD TV and Blu-ray Disc players, Notebook PCs and tablets, and home appliances.

Financial Highlights
(Currency in JPY)   **(Units: B = billion, M = million)**

	Mar. 2011	Mar. 2012	Mar. 2013	Mar. 2014	Mar. 2015
Revenue	6,398.50B	6,100.26B	5,800.28B	6,489.70B	6,655.89B
Gross profit	1,500.95B	1,465.06B	1,415.86B	1,623.91B	1,669.14B
Operating income	240,273M	202,663M	194,316M	257,126M	262,721M
Income before tax	195,549M	145,579M	155,553M	182,336M	136,644M
Net income	146,028M	71,349M	77,533M	68,942M	−37,825M
EBITDA	499,877M	452,309M	412,068M	428,922M	452,659M
Diluted EPS	31.25	16.32	18.31	14.23	−8.93
Dividends per share	5	8	8	8	4
Total assets	5,379.31B	5,752.73B	6,106.73B	6,172.51B	6,334.77B
Total liabilities	4,199.70B	4,522.52B	4,690.21B	4,726.52B	4,769.42B
Total equity	868,119M	863,481M	1,034.45B	1,027.18B	1,083.99B
Operating cash flow	374,084M	334,997M	132,316M	284,132M	330,442M

Source: Toshiba's home page, "Investor Relations", Higher Pay, Economic Growth Depend On New Markets, 10/5/2015, https://www.global.toshiba/ww/ir/corporate.html, accessed 1 August 2016.

Toshiba's Stock Prices for 2011–2015

Source: Yahoo Finance (n.d.), https://finance.yahoo.com/quote/tosbf/, accessed 1 August 2016.

payments were immediately suspended, and shareholders were left reeling.[8]

But where had these losses come from? An analysis of the now-accurate accounts traced a major portion of the loss back to the group's personal-computer and white-goods product lines, which accounted for JPY230bn (USD1.81bn) of the total losses.[9] This was attributed to Toshiba's strategic decision to shift the lion's share of the group's white-goods production overseas in the late 2000s, on the back of a strong yen. Unfortunately, the strategy backfired when the yen lost ground against other world currencies. In addition, competition from Toshiba's Asian rivals in the personal computer market contributed to operating losses of JPY109.7bn (USD0.87bn) in the fiscal year ending 31 March 2015. This represented a JPY54.6bn (USD0.43bn) decline from the year before.[10]

---

[8]Toshiba IR News (18 August 2015). "Notice Regarding Dividend of Surplus," http://www.toshiba.co.jp/about/ir/en/news/20150818_1.pdf, accessed 1 August 2016.
[9]*Ibid.*
[10]Supra note 7.

Fortunately, the firm's semiconductor business was thriving, due to high sales of smartphone flash memories, and this segment was propping up the rest of the firm.

The audit that followed Toshiba's accounting scandal revealed that, in addition to overstating profits, the firm had also conducted various write-downs. The actions of those involved were attributed to the fact that the group's executives had been placed under significant pressure following the 2011 Fukushima disaster, which seriously impacted Toshiba's nuclear unit.[11] In a bid to compensate for losses in this division, management had set aggressive targets in many other divisions, including smart meters and electronic toll booths, and this had led to executives inflating figures to create the impression that these difficult targets were being met.

Corporate checking and auditing systems that had come under scrutiny, following a 2011 accounting fraud scandal involving camera and medical device manufacturer Olympus Corp.,[12] were once again being brought into question as a result of the Toshiba case.[13] A major focus of the investigation into the accounting scandal centered on the roles that Toshiba's top officials played in the process, and the extent to which these highly respected professionals had been aware of the truth behind the figures. A fundamental requirement of the Corporate Governance Code of Japan implemented in June 2015 (see Exhibit 2) is that companies listed within the first and second sections of the Tokyo Stock Exchange must have at least two independent directors on their boards.[14] Toshiba had been fully compliant with this requirement. In fact, Toshiba had a model system in place, which was the envy of many similar firms, and the group had been one of the first organizations in Japan to offer places on its board to outsiders, with four of its 16 board members being independent representatives. However, it was later speculated that these members, two of

---

[11] Mainchi (31 August 2016). "What Happened for Toshiba?" http://mainichi.jp/premier/business/entry/index.html?id=20150831biz00m010032000c, accessed 1 August 2016.

[12] K.T. Greenfield (16 February 2012). "The Story behind the Olympus Scandal," *Bloomberg Businessweek*, http://www.businessweek.com/articles/2012-02-16/the-story-behind-the-olympusscandal, accessed 1 August 2016.

[13] For the details of the Olympus case, see D. Elam, M. Madrigal, and M. Jackson (2014). "Olympus Imaging Fraud Scandal: A Case Study," *AJBE American Journal of Business Education (AJBE)* 7(4). doi:10.19030/ajbe.v7i4.8812.

[14] Tokyo Stock Exchange (1 June 2015). "Corporate Governance Code," http://www.jpx.co.jp/equities/listing/cg/tvdivq0000008jdy-att/code.pdf, accessed 1 August 2016.

Exhibit 2:   New Corporate Governance Code of Japan[a]

On 1 June 2015, a new corporate governance code (Code) was introduced on the Tokyo Stock Exchange (TSE) under the patronage of the Financial Services Agency of the Japanese government. The Code represented a serious effort to reform the corporate governance systems systemic throughout Japan, which were frequently criticized for inhibiting growth and preventing boards of directors from being accountable to shareholders. While the new code was only applicable within publicly listed companies, the broad expectation was that the governance reforms that it promoted would ultimately shift to private companies.

The code outlined two basic approaches to corporate governance:

(1) **A Principle-Based Approach:** This approach required companies to consider each of five relevant principles, and to question whether its activities were in line with the spirit and purpose of these standards. In situations in which a discrepancy between the principle and the firm's operations were identified, the organization was required to take concrete actions to close this gap. The five principles were as follows:

   (i) **Securing the Rights and Equal Treatment of Shareholders:** In addition to securing shareholder rights and providing equal treatment for shareholders, companies should also give adequate consideration to the issues and concerns of minority and foreign shareholders. The Code also required companies listed on the first and second sections of the TSE to disclose any cross-shareholding positions they held in other companies, and the reasons why such cross-shareholding had been established.

   (ii) **Appropriate Cooperation with Stakeholders Other than Shareholders:** The Code emphasized the need for companies to recognize that their sustainable growth and mid-term or long-term corporate value were derived not only from the resources and contributions bestowed by shareholders, but also those provided by other stakeholders, such as employees and customers. It was essential that firms cooperate fully with all stakeholders.

   (iii) **Ensuring Appropriate Information Disclosure and Transparency:** As opposed to simply disclosing the bare minimum of information required by law and other regulations, under the Code, companies were expected to strive to actively provide information that went above and beyond what was required, if this was deemed to be important to the establishment of a constructive dialogue with shareholders.

   (iv) **Responsibilities of the Board:** The Code highlighted three main roles and responsibilities of the board of directors of a company: (1) setting the broad direction of corporate strategy; (2) establishing an environment in which appropriate risk-taking was supported; and (3) carrying out effective oversight of directors and management. The Code recommended that companies appoint a minimum of two independent directors to their boards.

Exhibit 2:   (*Continued*)

   (v) **Dialogue with Shareholders:** The Code recommended that companies enter into open, constructive dialogue with their shareholders, and that directors pay attention to shareholders' concerns and clearly explain the company's business policies to them.

(2) **Comply-or-Explain Approach:** This approach specified that, in the event a company did not comply with a principle, there was a requirement to explain the reasons for non-compliance in full and to be transparent with stakeholders and shareholders about any such non-compliance. This dialogue would ensure companies were held accountable for their actions and for failing to meet the required standards.

Note: [a]Financial Services Agency, Japan, (5 March 2015) "Corporate Governance Code" http://www.fsa.go.jp/singi/corporategovernance/, accessed 1 July 2016.

whom were former diplomats, may have lacked the skills and experience required to identify shortfalls in accounting practices.

Toshiba's Response to the Scandal

The accounting scandal rocked Toshiba to the core, and it was clear the organization faced a long and difficult road if it was to recover. On 17 September 2015, Masashi Muromachi, Representative Executive Officer, President, and CEO of Toshiba, issued a public apology to the organization's shareholders and stakeholders.[15] He sincerely apologized for the inconvenience and losses that Toshiba's actions had caused, and acknowledged that it would take time for the stakeholders and the public to regain their trust in, and respect for, Toshiba.[16] He vowed that Toshiba would return to the principles on which the organization had originally been formed, and that the Board would treat human life, safety, and compliance as the highest priorities in the forthcoming restructuring.[17] He promised he would personally endeavor to ensure that a new corporate culture was established that would prevent similar issues from ever

---

[15]Toshiba (17 September 2017). "Toshiba's New Management Team is Dedicated to Regaining Your Trust," http://www.toshiba.co.jp/worldwide/about/message.html, accessed 1 August 2016.

[16]*Ibid.*

[17]*Ibid.*

happening again.[18] Muromachi also disclosed plans to establish a Management Revitalization Committee consisting of outside experts and directors.[19] This committee would be tasked with facilitating the reform of corporate culture and identifying measures by which accounting irregularities could be prevented in the future.[20]

While Muromachi expressed his deep regret that the organization had taken so long to post the FY2014 financial results, he gave shareholders and customers his word that Toshiba would immediately begin the difficult task of restating the financial results for recent fiscal years, and that all accounting data would be submitted to the relevant authorities via the 176th Annual Securities Report.[21] Muromachi also promised to reinforce the audit function, implement new internal controls to enhance the corporate governance structure, and establish a new Internal Audit Division that would report to an Audit Committee consisting of independent outside directors.[22] To ensure top management was closely supervised and held accountable for their actions, he also vowed to increase the number of outside directors sitting on the Board of Directors to a majority, and to introduce a new evaluation system for the President and Chief Executive Officer (see Exhibit 3).[23]

Who Was Responsible for the Development of a Culture of Deception?

Toshiba's accounting practices could be traced back to the development of a high-pressure situation in which executives were expected to meet difficult targets in a challenging environment. This, in combination with the organization's top-down culture, which generated the expectation that

---

[18] *Ibid.*

[19] Toshiba (29 July 2015). "Notice on Action to Be Taken by Toshiba in Response to the Results of the Investigation Report by the Independent Investigation Committee," http://www.toshiba.co.jp/about/ir/en/news/20150729_1.pdf, accessed 1 August 2016.

[20] *Ibid.*

[21] Supra note 6.

[22] *Ibid.*

[23] *Ibid.*

Exhibit 3:   Toshiba's Actions Taken in Response to Inappropriate Accounting

8 Oct. 2015	Partial Restatement of Earnings Release for the Period Subject to Restatement of Past Financial Results: Restated Version Posted
17 Sept. 2015	Notice on Establishment of Executive-Liability Investigation Committee
14 Sept. 2015	Notice on Designation of Toshiba Shares as "Securities on Alert" and Imposition of Listing-Agreement Violation Penalty
9 Sept. 2015	Convocation Notice of the Extraordinary General Meeting of Shareholders
7 Sept. 2015	Notice on Restatement of Past Financial Results, FY2014 Consolidated Business Results, Submission of 176th Annual Securities Report and Outline of Recurrence Prevention Measures
7 Sept. 2015	Notice of Nominees for Directors, Committee Members, and Executive Officers
7 Sept. 2015	Notice of New Representative Executive Officers
7 Sept. 2015	Notice Regarding Holding of and Other Information on the Extraordinary General Meeting of Shareholders
31 Aug. 2015	Notice on Approval of Postponement (Re-extension) of the Deadline for Submission of the 176th Annual Securities Report (1 April 2014 to 31 March 2015)
18 Aug. 2015	Notices on Toshiba's New Management Team and Measures to Reform Governance Structure, and Outline of Correction of Past Financial Statements and Financial Forecast
29 Jul. 2015	Notice on Action to be taken by Toshiba in Response to the Results of the Investigation Report by the Independent Investigation Committee
21 Jul. 2015	Notice on Publication of the Full Version of the Investigation Report by the Independent Investigation Committee, Action to Be Taken by Toshiba, and Clarification of Managerial Responsibility
21 Jul. 2015	Notice on Appointment of Representative Executive Officers
20 Jul. 2015	Notice on Receiving Report from Independent Investigation Committee, and Action to Be Taken by Toshiba for Corrections Identified for Past Financial Results
25 Jun. 2015	Notice on Content of Matters to Be Reported at the Ordinary General Meeting of Shareholders for the 176th Fiscal Year
12 Jun. 2015	Notice on the Result of Self-check by Consolidated Subsidiaries, Outline of Investigation by Special Investigation Committee, and Relationship to Items Delegated to Independent Investigation Committee

(*Continued*)

Exhibit 3:   *(Continued)*

29 May 2015	Notice on Approval of Postponement of the Deadlines for Submission of the 176th Annual Securities Report (1 April 2014 to 31 March 2015) and the 177th First Quarterly Securities Report (1 April 2015 to 30 June 2015)
29 May 2015	Notice on Holding the Ordinary General Meeting of Shareholders
29 May 2015	Notice on Submission of Applications for Approval of Postponement of the Deadlines for Submission of the 176th Annual Securities Report (1 April 2014 to 31 March 2015) and the 177th First Quarterly Securities Report (1 April 2015 to 30 June 2015)
22 May 2015	Notice on Scope of Investigation by Independent Investigation Committee
15 May 2015	Notice on Selection of Members of Independent Investigation Committee
13 May 2015	Currently Expected Amount of Correction of Past Financial Results and Supplementary Explanation Regarding Independent Investigation Committee
8 May 2015	Notice Regarding Establishment of Independent Investigation Committee
8 May 2015	Notice Regarding Revision of Business Results Forecast
3 Apr. 2015	Notice Regarding Establishment of Special Investigation Committee

Source: Toshiba (1 August 2016). "Actions Taken in Response to Inappropriate Accounting," http://www.toshiba.co.jp/about/info-accounting/index.htm, accessed 1 August 2016.

employees should demonstrate blind loyalty to senior personnel, resulted in undesirable and illegal accounting practices' going unreported.[24] While senior executives were quick to deny that they had purposely delayed the process through which losses were booked, their subordinates were solidly of the opinion that delayed booking of losses had been conducted at their managers' instructions.[25] At the monthly meetings that were attended by the heads of in-house companies and subsidiaries, top management issued "challenges" and earnings improvement targets to their teams and

---

[24]Toshiba (21 July 2015). "Notice on Publication of the Full Version of the Investigation Report by the Independent Investigation Committee, Action to Be Taken by Toshiba, and Clarification of Managerial Responsibility," http://www.toshiba.co.jp/about/ir/en/news/20151208_2.pdf, accessed 1 August 2016.

[25]*Ibid.*

urged employees to "get creative" to ensure such targets were met.[26] These targets were particularly aggressive in the 2011 and 2012 fiscal years.[27] The resulting pressure engendered a culture of deceit. Essentially, Toshiba's failings were not due solely to a lack of corporate governance or poor internal controls; they were the direct result of the actions of a wayward corporate management team.[28] To prevent any future accounting scandals, it was critical that Toshiba's new management team take positive action to eradicate the dishonest and profit-driven corporate culture that had emerged.

Accounting figures represent the most important measurement by which shareholders can determine how a company is performing. The people who invested money in Toshiba did so on the basis of the figures in the firm's annual report, and the assumption was that these figures were honest and accurate. Once the full extent of the deception was unveiled, it became apparent that Toshiba had a serious problem. Irregular accounting practices were not limited to just one or two rogue divisions within the organization, but had become a standard part of the group's operating practices, and were conducted systematically across the firm.[29] As opposed to being limited to the infrastructure division, where the problems were first unearthed, inaccurate accounting methods were found in the majority of Toshiba's principal business divisions, including the semiconductor, computer, and television businesses.

The propensity for staff to massage the figures could be traced back to Toshiba's strong top-down culture, which discouraged staff from questioning the authority of senior management. The extent to which the culture was corrupt and employees were programmed to do as they were told was evidenced by the fact that, in some cases, the illegal deception had been going on for as long as eight years, without a single employee blowing the whistle.[30] Every manager throughout the organization, from middle management up to the president, had his or her eye firmly on profit.

---

[26] *Ibid.*

[27] *Ibid.*

[28] *Ibid.*

[29] According to the third-party panel report. See *Japan Times* (16 May 2015). "Third-Party Panel to Probe Toshiba Bookkeeping," http://www.japantimes.co.jp/news/2015/05/16/business/corporate-business/third-party-panel-to-probe-toshiba-bookkeeping/#.V2ZAd7grJ2Q, accessed 1 July 2016.

[30] *Ibid.*

Manipulating figures and inflating earnings had become so systematic throughout the organization that it was practically impossible for any one employee to overturn this illegal practice.[31] The only way forward was to change the firm's top-down culture by completely restructuring the management team[32] (see Exhibit 4). It was clear that the numerous controls and systems that were in place were insufficient in themselves. They also depended on the development of a culture that fostered and supported honest reporting.

Was Corporate Governance an Illusion?

I myself tried hard to make significant changes to Toshiba's image. Clearly, I didn't try hard enough.

— Taizo Nishimuro, President of Japan Post Holdings Co.,
Toshiba president during the late 1990s[33]

Toshiba had once been considered to be a pioneer in corporate governance. The company began a process of reform in the late 1990s, which continued into the new millennium. In 1998, it created a corporate officer system that transformed the company management into something that more closely resembled a US-type management model, with a committee governance framework. The creation of a committee governance structure increased the authority of the external board members who formed the majority of the three separate management committees responsible for appointing board members and overseeing management. Toshiba's strong external scrutiny should have been an example of an advanced, robust system of corporate governance. Unfortunately, in 2008, Toshiba, led by the president and other senior company executives, began a drive to achieve profit targets above all other considerations. This behavior was unimpeded by corporate governance controls and led to the company booking JPY150bn in overstated profits. While internal board members

---

[31] *Ibid.*

[32] *Ibid.*

[33] Mainichi (25 July 2015). "Toshiba Scandal Shows Company Had Illusion of Corporate Governance," http://mainichi.jp/english/english/features/news/20150723p2a00m0na 012000c.html, accessed 1 August 2016.

Exhibit 4: Cultural Differences between US and Japanese Companies

	US	Japan
Board Members	Elected representatives. Less than 15 people per board.	Representatives who have been promoted internally. Can be more than 30 people per board.
Company Objective	To maximize shareholder wealth.	To maximize stakeholder wealth. Shareholders are considered to be as important as management, employees, suppliers, and customers.
Agency Problem	Managers typically pursue their own objectives and act in their own interests. Performance and behavior are typically influenced by incentives to maximize shareholder wealth.	The objectives of the stakeholders can be varied and dynamic. As such, the agency problem is more complicated.
Employment	Transient.	Lifetime and seniority-based. Employees typically progress according to seniority.
Speed vs. Consistency	Rapid and efficient decision-making approaches are favored.	Company makes decisions in stages in accordance with the wider corporate hierarchy. Management is typically conservative in their decision-making processes and takes a significant amount of time to make a decision.
Heterogeneous vs. Homogeneous	Heterogeneous. The US is multicultural; as such, people think in very different ways. Flexibility and openness to new ideas are encouraged.	Homogeneous. The majority of people come from the same background and have worked for the same firm for a long period of time.
Collaboration	Efficiency is highly valued. The fewer and less time-consuming the meetings are, the better.	Meetings are a standard part of daily work life and can be lengthy.
Remote vs. Face-to-Face Communications	Communications are typically more remote, and email and phone calls are preferred over meeting face to face.	Meetings are generally conducted on a face-to-face basis.
Personal Life vs. Professional Life	Family and personal time are treated as a priority. Work–life balance is highly valued.	Work takes priority over family and personal life.

(*Continued*)

Exhibit 4:   *(Continued)*

Self-sponsored vs. Company-sponsored Retirement Rewards	People pursue their own objectives, and this means they will readily leave a firm if a better career opportunity is presented elsewhere. As such, turnover tends to be relatively high.	People tend to stay in one company and are encouraged to do so through monetary rewards and seniority-based promotion mechanisms.

Hofstede Cultural Analysis

Power/Distance	Power is typically evenly distributed among managers at each hierarchical level. Lower-level managers may challenge the decisions of their superiors.	Top-down: Power is unequally distributed. Top management personnel make all the decisions and pass them down to lower-level personnel, who are expected to carry out all orders.
Individualism/ Collectivism	Individuals should make a positive contribution that is aligned with the company goals. However, members are typically self-centered and competitive, as opposed to cooperative. Employees are not typically loyal to the organizations they work for, and will pursue their own goals. They do not depend on others and can be calculating and strategic in their behavior.	The group takes precedence over the individual. Members of the group must act for the greater good of the whole, as opposed to in their own interests. As such, employees strongly subscribe to the perspective that joint efforts reap group rewards.
Masculinity/ Femininity	Women and men work together. Small is considered to be beautiful, and high value is placed on caring for the environment and having a good quality of life.	The culture is masculine. Women and men have segregated roles. Big is considered to be good. Money is highly valued, and people like to show off power and wealth.
Uncertainty Avoidance	Uncertainties are managed as they arise and without undue anxiety. People may agree to do something even if they are not 100% confident that it is possible.	Members do not like uncertainty. It is only in situations in which they are 100% confident that they can achieve something that they will say "yes."
Long-Term vs. Short-Term Orientation	Short-term	Long-term

were certainly privy to some critical information about the true performance of the firm, the delayed losses went unnoticed by external board
members.[34]

The issues with fraudulent accounting practices exposed the weak-
nesses in Toshiba's corporate governance model, especially with respect
to the appointment of external board members.[35] Two of the four external
board members were former diplomats who had little experience of management and accounting practices, and a poor grasp of finance and law.[36]
It appeared they were appointed only to reach target numbers, as opposed
to providing serious management oversight. Toshiba's much-acclaimed
corporate governance system was subsequently exposed as being nothing
more than illusory (see Exhibit 5).

Goodwill Impairment Related to Westinghouse Electric

*I will take the lead and disclose information more actively to gain trust
from stakeholders. We feel deeply responsible for our failure to publicize
the huge write-downs, considering that investors have strong interest in
Westinghouse's business.*

— Masashi Muromachi, Toshiba President[37]

On 17 October 2006, Toshiba, which was Japan's largest manufacturer of
nuclear power-plant equipment at the time, purchased Westinghouse
Electric Co., allowing it to acquire BNFL USA Group Inc. and
Westinghouse UK Limited (collectively: Westinghouse) for a purchase
price of USD5.4bn.[38]

---

[34] *Ibid.*

[35] *Ibid.*

[36] *Ibid.*

[37] Muromachi held a press conference on 17 November 2015, only after the Tokyo Stock
Exchange urged him to do so. For the details, see Nikkei (17 November 2015). "Toshiba
President Vows Greater Transparency in Wake of Serial Scandal," http://asia.nikkei.com/
Business/Companies/Toshiba-president-vows-greater-transparency-in-wake-of-serial-
scandal, accessed 1 August 2016.

[38] Toshiba (17 October 2006). "Toshiba Completes Westinghouse Acquisition," http://
www.toshiba.co.jp/about/ir/en/news/20061017_2.htm, accessed 1 August 2016.

Exhibit 5:   The Difference between Corporate Governance Practices in Japan and the US

Although they share some basic similarities, the board structures and governance practices of US and Japanese businesses differ significantly. These differences have become particularly more noticeable in the process of SEC-mandated reforms such as independent audit and compensation committees.

US Corporate Governance Practices Required of NYSE-Listed Companies	Japanese Governance Practices as Mandated by the Japanese Company Act
Section 303A of the NYSE Listed Company Manual outlines the independence requirements for all NYSE-listed US companies. According to this directive, all firms must have a majority of directors who meet independence requirements.	Under the Companies Act of Japan, there is no requirement for a company that adopts the structure of the three committees to have a majority of outside directors on the board; however, all firms are required to have a majority of external directors on every audit, nomination, and compensation committee.
All NYSE-listed US companies must ensure that an audit committee is in place which consists of at least three members. This committee must meet the requirements of Section 303A of the NYSE Listed Company Manual, including those imposed by Rule 10A-3 under the US Securities Exchange Act of 1934. Every member of the audit committee should be an independent director.	If a Japanese company has an audit committee that consists of three directors, two of these need to be outside directors in order to ensure that the firm complies with the requirements of the Companies Act of Japan.

According to Section 303A of the NYSE Listed Company Manual, all NYSE-listed US companies must have a nominating/corporate governance committee in place that consists of independent directors. The responsibilities of this committee should be outlined in full.	To comply with the Companies Act of Japan, Japanese firms need to have a nomination committee in place that consists of three directors, two of whom should be external directors.
According to Section 303 A.02(a)(ii) of the NYSE Listed Company Manual, NYSE-listed organizations are required to have a compensation committee in place which consists entirely of independent directors. These committee members are permitted to access advice from other advisors, providing the process they follow to gain such advice is in compliance with prescribed independence criteria.	The Companies Act of Japan requires Japanese companies to have an established compensation committee that consists of three directors, two of whom are outside directors.
Generally speaking, all NYSE-listed US companies must obtain the approval of shareholders prior to issuing any equity compensation plan.	According to the Companies Act of Japan, stock options represent compensation for the services that company directors and executives have performed. As such, they are not subject to shareholder approval.
All external directors of an NYSE-listed US organization must meet at regularly scheduled executive sessions, in the absence of management.	Under the Companies Act of Japan, there is no requirement for outside directors to meet without the presence of inside directors.

Through integrating Westinghouse and its extensive expertise in nuclear power into Toshiba, the organization was able to develop a global energy-systems perspective, and position itself as the world's leading nuclear power organization. At that time, the nuclear power industry was very attractive due to renewed interest throughout the world in nuclear energy and environment-friendly technologies. China and many other developing economies had already invested heavily in plant construction, and the need for additional nuclear energy capacity was emerging in the United States and Europe. At the time, there were 439 nuclear power plants operating around the world, and demand for additional nuclear energy was poised to grow as part of the more environmentally conscious society of the 21st century.

At the time of the merger, Toshiba was a leader in BWR[39] technology in the Japanese market, while Westinghouse enjoyed a leading position in the world market with its PWR[40] nuclear systems. Through combining the competing offerings of Toshiba and Westinghouse, the organization was able to leverage its manufacturing, sales and marketing, engineering, and R&D capabilities. It was anticipated that the merger would enable Toshiba to develop a major strategic advantage in the nuclear sector and technological synergies allowing the firm to enter new business areas. In addition, the merger was expected to boost sales by up to JPY700bn by 2015 and JPY900bn by 2020, a JPY700bn increase over current sales.[41]

However, despite initial high hopes, by 2015 it became clear that Toyota's merger with Westinghouse had not delivered on its anticipated advantages. Following the 2011 nuclear disaster in Fukushima, interest in nuclear technology had waned significantly, and Westinghouse had been forced to book impairment losses. In 2012 alone, Westinghouse booked losses of USD900mn, followed by a further USD400mn in 2013.[42] These results were devastating for Toshiba in light of the fact that

---

[39]BWR: Boiling Water Reactor, a reactor developed and commercialized by General Electric in the US.

[40]PWR: Pressurized Water Reactor, a reactor developed and commercialized by Westinghouse in the US.

[41]Toshiba (17 November 2015). "Regarding Goodwill Impairment Related to Toshiba's Consolidated Subsidiary, Westinghouse Electric Company L.L.C.," http://www.toshiba.co.jp/about/ir/index.htm, accessed 1 August 2016.

[42]*Ibid.*

the firm had invested USD5.4bn in the acquisition of an 87% stake in Westinghouse.[43]

It is standard accounting practice that, when an acquired company becomes less profitable than it was at the time of acquisition, the parent firm should reduce the goodwill value in their own books to ensure that the true value of the investment is represented. In short, Toshiba was legally obliged to report Westinghouse's USD1.3bn write-downs to the public and investors.[44] However, it failed to do so, in violation of the rules of the Tokyo Stock Exchange.[45] Toshiba explained its actions as follows: "Impairment testing is conducted for the overall business results of Westinghouse and the division of Toshiba responsible for Westinghouse. Because the division as a whole was profitable, no goodwill impairment was necessary."[46] However, these events had already started to throw Toshiba's accounting practices into doubt.

On 27 November 2015, Toshiba executives promised investors that the organization would adopt greater transparency in their accounting practices and that they would actively disclose information to the public in a more timely and accurate manner.[47] Toshiba also notified the Tokyo Stock Exchange of Westinghouse's fiscal 2012 and 2013 write-downs of JPY115.6bn (USD0.925bn).[48]

Legal and Administrative Implications for Toshiba

The first disclosure of accounting issues at Toshiba came on 3 April 2015, when the company issued a press release announcing that an independent committee was to be established to carry out a special investigation into

---

[43] *Ibid.*
[44] *Ibid.*
[45] *Ibid.*
[46] Supra note 37.
[47] *Ibid.*
[48] Supra note 41.

accounting practices on certain infrastructure projects.[49] Investor confidence in Toshiba was severely damaged by these revelations and the stock price collapsed by 26% following the news, prompting shareholders to seek damages for the losses incurred (see Exhibit 1).[50]

(1) Shareholders' class action against the company: Class action legal proceedings were brought against the company by those who had purchased shares of Toshiba between 8 May 2012 and 7 May 2015 (known as the "Class Period"), with the Court serving as the lead plaintiff.[51] According to the complaint, during the Class Period, the defendants had made false and/or misleading statements. They also argued:

(i)   The total amounts of contract costs for certain infrastructure projects were underestimated;

(ii) The timing with which such contract losses were recorded was improper; and

(iii) Toshiba's public statements were materially false and misleading.[52]

(2) Administrative actions against Toshiba: Once the independent investigation had concluded, Toshiba faced hefty financial penalties from regulators. The Securities and Exchange Surveillance Commission (SESC) and the Financial Services Agency of Japan deliberated administrative disciplinary action against Toshiba.[53] As a consequence of the investigation, the Tokyo Stock Exchange placed Toshiba on a watch list of companies with poor or inadequate internal controls.[54] Based on the commission's decision, the FSA's Certified Public Accountants and

---

[49] *Ibid.*

[50] *Ibid.*

[51] Mainichi (5 September 2015). "Class Action for Toshiba?" http://mainichi.jp/select/news/20150906k0000m040045000c.html, accessed 1 August 2016.

[52] *Ibid.*

[53] Toshiba (12 July 2015). "Notice on Recommendation for Administrative Monetary Penalty Payment Order by the Securities and Exchange Surveillance Commission," https://www.toshiba.co.jp/about/ir/en/news/20151207_2.pdf, accessed 1 August 2016.

[54] Toshiba IR News (14 September 2015). "Notice on Designation of Toshiba Shares as 'Securities on Alert' and Imposition of Listing Agreement Violation Penalty," http://www.toshiba.co.jp/about/ir/en/news/20150914_1.pdf, accessed 1 August 2016.

Auditing Oversight Board also investigated Ernst & Young Shin Nihon, the auditing company that had signed off on Toshiba's earnings.[55]

(3) Toshiba's legal action against former executives: In September 2015, Toshiba set up an external panel of three lawyers to examine whether former executives had fulfilled their basic duties when the accounting malpractices were in full swing. On 25 October 2015, after an independent panel's report on the company's book-padding scandal was released, Toshiba initiated legal action against former executives, including presidents Hisao Tanaka, Atsutoshi Nishida, and Norio Sasaki.[56] Japanese corporate law stipulated that company executives were liable for any damages their companies suffer as a result of their failings.[57] Toshiba filed a civil case against 28 current and former executives for damaging the company's reputation, and sued for a total of JPY1bn (USD8.2mn) in compensatory damages.[58] Toshiba's decision to sue the former executives was driven by shareholder demands that former executives be held accountable for the book-padding that had taken place.

(4) Could Clawback Provisions Come into Play? Although there is no "clawback" (or recovery) law in Japan itself, some Japanese corporations listed in the United States are subject to statutory clawback provisions for certain employees, and this was the case for Toshiba. Clawback could take several forms, such as applying to vested as well as unvested awards, annual bonuses, long-term equity incentives, and even non-equity compensation. They may be triggered by misconduct or poor financial performance.

---

[55] *Ibid.*

[56] Mainichi (25 October 2015). "Toshiba Preparing to Sue Former Executives," 2016, http://www.nikkei.com/article/DGXLASDZ24H5Q_U5A021C1MM8000/?dg=1, accessed 1 August 2016. And also see Toshiba (7 December 2015). "Notice on Action for Compensatory Damages against Former Company Executives," http://www.toshiba.co.jp/about/ir/en/news/20151207_3.pdf, accessed 1 August 2016.

[57] Japanese Corporation Law Article 423, https://liblawuw.libguides.com/c.php?g=1239338&p=9069990, accessed 1 August 2016.

[58] Toshiba (27 January 2016). "Notice on Petition for Increase in Amount Sought in Action for Compensatory Damages against Former Company Executives on the Grounds of Toshiba's Payment of Administrative Monetary Penalty, etc.," http://www.toshiba.co.jp/about/ir/en/news/20160127_2.pdf, accessed 1 August 2016.

Following the US financial crisis of 2007–2008, Wall Street regulators and politicians forced banks to adopt so-called clawback provisions in order to recover the compensation paid to banking executives whose longer-term deals incurred losses. A key feature of the crisis was the lack of accountability of traders whose deals had been profitable in the short-term, and who had subsequently been paid generous performance-related compensation, despite the fact that the trades incurred significant losses at later dates. Following its implementation on Wall Street, the Dodd–Frank law passed by the US Congress obliged all listed companies to implement clawback provisions on executives for up to three years following payment of compensation.[59]

In theory, the rule was designed to ensure executives were held accountable. If a company had made less than its stated earnings and an executive had been paid on those earnings, it would make perfect sense for the firm to clawback the compensation. As such, it was envisaged that the rule would go a long way toward preventing executives from being inappropriately rewarded. However, the reality was very different from the theory. The fundamental issue with the Dodd–Frank law was that the legal requirements were frequently misinterpreted. In addition, instead of controlling how much executives were paid, the law served to increase base salaries, because executives demanded compensation for the risk of potential clawback. This reduced the incentive for executives to maximize profits and, therefore, they were not necessarily acting in the shareholders' best interests. Furthermore, the new rule was unique because it specified that recoveries were to be made regardless of whether fault could be attributed to an individual executive. In addition, it applied to a broad group of people that included not only senior officers, but also to any other employee who had responsibility for policy-making exercises.

The Dodd–Frank law strictly prohibited US companies from indemnifying or reimbursing any executives subject to clawbacks. However, the law did allow a firm the option of not pursuing a clawback if it anticipated that the costs associated with doing so would outweigh the amount that could be recovered. But could Toshiba sue their executive managers to make them accountable for their financial reporting practices on this basis?

---

[59]The White House (n.d.). "Wall Street Reform: The Dodd–Frank Act," https://www.archives.gov/presidential-libraries/archived-websites, accessed 1 August 2016.

Decision for the New CEO

I want to step aside within three years once things settle down somewhat
so that younger hands can devote themselves to a strategy for growth.

— Masashi Muromachi, Toshiba CEO[60]

On 21 July 2015, Masashi Muromachi was appointed Toshiba's new president and CEO. The organization was at a crossroads in its history, and it was imperative that the new CEO have the strong strategic, corporate, and social qualities needed to drive real organizational change.[61] Toshiba set sail on rough seas with a new board of executives. At a special shareholders' meeting that was held in Tokyo on 30 September 2015, Toshiba added seven outsiders, including Shiseido senior adviser Shinzo Maeda and Mitsubishi Chemical Holdings chairman Yoshimitsu Kobayashi, to its board. However, the future still looked uncertain.[62] Unprofitable businesses that had been propped up by accounting maneuvers remained intact. President Muromachi told shareholders that the company would not hesitate to streamline the personal computer, television, white-goods, and semiconductor businesses, with memory chips being the exception.[63] Fine words, indeed. But was Toshiba following through on these promises? Many managers had stepped down as a result of the scandal, and Toshiba faced many challenges to overcome if it was to ever get back on its feet.[64]

President Muromachi approached the momentous task by investigating how the situation had been allowed to arise in the first place[65]:

---

[60]Mainichi (5 September 2015). "Class Action for Toshiba?" http://mainichi.jp/select/news/20150906k0000m040045000c.html, accessed 1 August 2016.

[61]Toshiba (21 December 2015). "Toshiba to Execute 'Toshiba Revitalization Action Plan,'" http://www.toshiba.co.jp/about/ir/en/news/20151221_4.pdf, accessed 1 August 2016.

[62]Toshiba (20 September 2015). "Notice of Resolutions, The Extraordinary General Meeting of Shareholders (30 September 2015)," http://www.toshiba.co.jp/about/ir/en/stock/pdf/tsm2015e_resol.pdf, accessed 1 August 2016.

[63]*Ibid.*

[64]*Ibid.*

[65]Toshiba (2015). "Annual Report," https://www.annualreports.com/HostedData/AnnualReportArchive/t/OTC_TOSYY_2015.pdf, accessed 1 August 2016. And also see, Muromachi held a press conference on 17 November 2015 only after the Tokyo Stock

Exhibit 6: **Differences between Internal and External Auditors**

Focus	Internal Auditors	External Auditors
Appointment	Employees of the company.	External resource that is appointed on behalf of the board of directors.
Objectives	Set by management. May be limited to certain areas of the organization.	Defined by statute and regulations. Have free rein to examine all systems and processes throughout the organization.
Responsibility	Responsible to senior managers.	Responsible to the company's owners, the shareholders, the government, and the general public.

(1) Why had the corporate governance structures that were in place at Toshiba failed to work? Were there inherent problems in the attitude and approach taken by the company's top management? Why hadn't the corporate governance structures and reforms that Toshiba had implemented been more closely aligned with those that had been proven to work in the US and Europe? Were there considerable differences between corporate governance practices in Japan and the US?

(2) Toshiba had a corporate governance system in place to keep a close eye on management. Why had internal and external audit functions failed at Toshiba (see Exhibit 6)?

(3) Had Toshiba failed in its objectives to create a transparency forum? How effective was Toshiba's fraud-resistant corporate ecology or culture?

(4) Through the implementation of aggressive targets that were disguised as "challenges," and calls for employees to "get creative," had Toshiba actively fostered a top-down corporate process of deceit?

(5) To what extent were Toshiba's failings the result of the lifetime employment and seniority systems that were common in Japan?

The huge responsibility of getting the company back on track and restoring the brand's reputation rested heavily on the shoulders of Masashi

---

Exchange urged him to do so. For the details, see Nikkei (17 November 2015). "Toshiba President Vows Greater Transparency in Wake of Serial Scandal," https://www.bbc.com/news/business-33605638, accessed 1 August 2016.

Muromachi.[66] Muromachi had a long way to go to restore the trust that had been lost as a result of the accounting scandal. He was also well aware that the brand's reputation had been significantly damaged and that this would, in itself, entail further sales losses.

Ensuring that the organization benefited from diverse and varied revenue sources had been an area of weakness for Toshiba for quite some time and, following the scandal, it was imperative that Toshiba immediately restructure its entire household appliances division. The former president, Hisao Tanaka, had previously claimed that the organization was taking active steps to reduce its reliance on the electronic devices and components market.[67] However, in reality, the firm's dependence on this market was much higher than disclosed. This failing was compounded by the failure of its overseas manufacturing strategy. Although Toshiba's executives had attempted to counter the impact of the falling yen by placing a strategic focus on more advanced, value-added products, this strategy had also failed. In the fiscal year ending March 2015, the firm sustained a JPY39bn impairment loss.

A further issue was that the firm's rivals were reporting strong results. In the 2015 fiscal year, Hitachi was expected to announce an operating profit for the third successive year.[68] Mitsubishi had also reported the strong performance of its factory-automation equipment.[69] Mitsubishi had strategically enhanced revenue from its consumer appliances division by focusing on high-performing products such as air conditioners, rice cookers, and refrigerators.[70] In addition to unloading ineffective assets, it would be crucial that Toshiba streamline its operations in the future. Now was the time for Toshiba to transform the less competitive business segments that had directly contributed to the process by which earnings manipulation had permeated the organization. There was an inherent need for Toshiba to completely reassess its Southeast Asian white-goods operations and to re-examine its semiconductor business in terms of both its

---

[66] *Ibid.*

[67] Nikkei (21 June 2015). "Toshiba's Accounting Scandal," http://www.nikkei.com/article/DGXZZO89536830R20C15A7000000/, accessed 1 August 2016.

[68] *Ibid.*

[69] *Ibid.*

[70] *Ibid.*

system and discrete chip segments.[71] Furthermore, there was a fundamental need for a shift in focus from corporate offerings to consumer products in the personal-computer division.[72]

Muromachi identified a number of key responsibilities that would be of major importance for the new CEO of Toshiba[73]:

(1) Developing, sharing, and implementing Toshiba's vision, mission, and strategy. Formalizing a strategic direction through which the plan's main deliverables could be achieved.

Prior to the accounting scandal, managers and executives throughout Toshiba had been operating under significant pressure from top management to achieve target profits. Unable to meet such stringent "challenges," many of the managers had resorted to massaging the figures and delaying losses. The culture of the organization was fundamentally to blame, and it was now imperative that this culture undergo significant reform. The accounting scandal had exposed Toshiba's structure of corporate governance as something that lacked credibility and substance. But how could Muromachi change something that had evolved over many, many years?[74]

(2) Managing the organization and value chain according to the requirements specified in strategic plans. Ensuring the work and behavior of executive leaders, both internal and external, were aligned with corporate objectives.

Toshiba faced numerous accusations that the executive management committee had not followed effective processes when selecting external board members.[75] The future external board members needed to possess advanced knowledge of law, finance, and accounting. However, Muromachi was undecided as to whether Toshiba should rely on the four external board members to ensure adequate corporate governance was

---

[71] *Ibid.*

[72] *Ibid.*

[73] Toshiba IR News (3 April 2015). "Notice Regarding Establishment of Special Investigation Committee," http://www.toshiba.co.jp/worldwide/index.html, accessed 1 August 2016.

[74] *Ibid.*

[75] *Ibid.*

exercised, or insist that this task was the responsibility of internal board members, who had advanced, internal knowledge of Toshiba.

(3) Devising, communicating, and implementing a strategic business plan that guided the development and direction of the organization. Ensuring management strategies and standards that took the competitive landscape, opportunities, and threats in the external market, and developments in the market and industry, into account.

Muromachi pursued a no-holds-barred approach to structural reform, and nothing was off limits. Toshiba could shut down any white-goods manufacturing plants that were located abroad and reorganize the overseas network of factories that were producing large appliances.[76] Some 90% of Toshiba's large appliances were made in China, Indonesia, and Thailand, yet importing refrigerators, washing machines, and other items to sell in Japan had become far less profitable than it once was. However, this was not the sole reason for Toshiba's demise.[77] The firm's poor performance was also rooted in the competitiveness of its products.[78] Muromachi knew that Toshiba had fallen behind other companies in terms of the speed at which it brought new offerings to market.[79] In light of the fact that Toshiba could pull out of some markets altogether, he believed that an unbiased decision should be made about what to do with the domestic white-goods, television, and personal-computer (PC) businesses. Although Toshiba had once been a dominant player in the PC market, having launched the world's first mass-market laptop computer, its market share had declined in recent years as a result of the increase in competition from lower-cost manufacturers from mainland China and China Taiwan.[80] He very much saw his responsibility as planting the seeds of growth. It was then up to his successors to make these seeds prosper and grow. But where exactly should he plant these seeds?

---

[76] *Ibid.*
[77] *Ibid.*
[78] *Ibid.*
[79] *Ibid.*
[80] *Ibid.*

For Further Discussion

(1) What could Toshiba have done differently after the accounting scandal was uncovered?

(2) Can corporate scandals such as the one that arose in Toshiba be linked to the lifetime employment system that is typical in Japanese organizations?

(3) How can companies create a fraud-resistant corporate ecology or culture?

(4) How important is it that firms create a transparency forum? How does the Toshiba case support this view?

(5) In what ways are Japan and the US different culturally? What elements of Japan's culture contributed to Toshiba's downfall?

(6) Why did Toshiba's internal audit function fail?

(7) Internal vs. external auditors: How can auditors effectively detect company fraud?

Case 3

Interest-Rate Swap Offered by Sumitomo Mitsui Bank: Was This for Hedging or Speculation?*

Sumitomo Mitsui Banking Corporation (the Bank) was found to have breached its duty of explanation when an interest-rate swap agreement was executed between the Bank and a customer (the Company), under which fixed and floating interest rates would be swapped and the resulting difference settled (see Exhibit 1).[1]

*Professor Mitsuru Misawa prepared this case for class discussion. Dr. Misawa is a professor of finance and director of the Center for Japanese Global Investment and Finance at the University of Hawaii at Manoa. This case is not intended to show effective or ineffective handling of decision or business processes. The authors might have disguised certain information to protect confidentiality. Cases are written in the past tense, this is not meant to imply that all practices, organizations, people, places or fact mentioned in the case no longer occur, exist or apply.
[1]Fukuoka District Court, 24 June 2008, 2006 (wa) No. 71, Fukuoka High Court, 27 April 2011, 2008 (ne) No. 658 and the Supreme Court, 7 March 2013, 2011 (ju) No. 1493. For the Supreme Court decision, see http://www.courts.go.jp/app/hanrei_jp/detail2?id=83047, accessed 21 September 2016.

Exhibit 1:   Sumitomo Mitsui Banking Corporation

Sumitomo Mitsui Banking Corporation (SMBC) was established in April 2001 through the merger of two leading banks: The Sakura Bank, Limited, and The Sumitomo Bank, Limited. Sumitomo Mitsui Financial Group, Inc., was established in December 2002 through a stock transfer as a bank holding company, and SMBC became a wholly owned subsidiary of SMFG. In March 2003, SMBC merged with the Wakashio Bank, Ltd. SMBC's competitive advantages included a strong customer base, the quick implementation of strategies, and an extensive lineup of financial products and services that leveraged the expertise of strategic Group companies in specialized areas. SMBC, as a core member of SMFG, worked together with other members of the Group to offer customers highly sophisticated, comprehensive financial services.

Company Name:	Sumitomo Mitsui Banking Corporation		
Business Profile:	Banking		
Establishment:	6 June 1996		
Head Office:	1–2, Marunouchi 1-chome, Chiyoda-ku, Tokyo		
Employees:	28,002 (as of 31 March 2016)		
Network:	Domestic	branches:	440
	Overseas	branches:	17
	(as of 31 March 2016)		

Business Profile
O   Deposit taking
O   Lending
O   Securities retail sales and trading
O   Securities investment
O   Fund transfer
O   Foreign exchange
O   Insourcing of financial futures transactions
O   Corporate bond trustee and custody services
O   Trust bank business (money claim trustee services related to asset securitization business)
O   Investment trust sales
O   Securities intermediary business
O   Retail sales of insurance products

Source: SMFG Home Page, https://www.smfg.co.jp/investor/stock/overview.html.

Background

The Company was a corporation that managed pachinko parlors. On 30 December 2003,[2] the Company borrowed JPY1.5bn from the Bank,

---

[2]USD1 = JPY106.96 on 30 December 2003.

which was the Company's main financial institution. The loan was made under the condition that a variable interest rate of 0.75% per annum would be added to the Tokyo Interbank Offering Rate (TIBOR). When the loan was made, Mr. Arai, a Bank employee, knew that the Company had often borrowed from other banks under variable-interest-rate conditions. Mr. Arai suggested the transaction in question as an instrument to hedge against risk associated with rising interest rates.

The transaction in question was an interest-rate swap agreement. That is, based on an agreement between the concerned parties, a certain notional principal and a transaction period were set and fixed, variable interest rates swapped in the same currency, and the resulting difference settled. This was a simple "plain vanilla interest-rate swap" deal. Such a swap could be further categorized as either a spot-start swap, under which transactions commenced simultaneously with the execution of the agreement, or a forward-start swap, under which transactions commenced after a certain period following the execution of the agreement had elapsed.

On 19 January 2004, Mr. Arai issued Mr. Ko, the Company's representative director, a written proposal titled "Guidance for interest-rate swap agreement (hedging against the risk of rising financing costs)" and explained the transaction system.

Mr. Ko requested that Mr. Arai explain descriptions in the written proposal in the presence of Mr. Daiwa, who was a Company advisory tax accountant. On 28 January 2004, Mr. Arai issued Mr. Ko and Mr. Daiwa a written proposal including information on and explanations of the two types of interest-rate swap agreements — spot-start and forward-start.

On 23 February 2004, Mr. Ko stated that he would reply a few days after he had confirmed opinions received from Mr. Daiwa and Mr. Miyashita, the Company's president. In March 2004, assuming that the variable interest rate would not rise in the near future, Mr. Ko opted for an interest-rate swap agreement in which transactions would commence in one year.

On 3 March 2004, Mr. Arai issued a written proposal, including relevant information about the interest-rate swap agreement under which transactions would commence in one year, and again provided relevant explanation. He explained that a specific contractual fixed interest rate would be reported the following day, and the agreement would be established upon Mr. Ko approving such an interest rate. Mr. Ko signed and affixed the Company seal in the space of the written proposal, labeled: "I have received explanations from your bank upon application for the interest-rate swap agreement in question, and I hereby confirm that I understand the relevant transaction's risks."

On 4 March 2004, Mr. Arai contacted Mr. Ko, mentioning that the fixed interest rate would be 2.445% per annum, and obtained approval. The agreement in question was executed between the Bank and the Company on 4 March 2004.

The agreement in question had set JPY300mn as a notional principal, and the fixed interest rate payment and floating interest rate payment, as set forth in what follows, would be swapped and paid on the eighth day of the third month following 8 June 2005, and every third month thereafter during the transaction period from 8 March 2005 to 8 March 2011. In addition, the expression "TIBOR" in the contract was confirmed as referring to "Tokyo Interbank Offering Rates," the interest rates used by banks in the Tokyo market when they lent funds to other banks. The contractual terms of payment were:

Terms of payment by the Company to the Bank for the fixed interest rate: 2.445% per annum
Terms of payment by the Bank to the Company for the floating interest rate: 3-month TIBOR + 0%

During the period from 8 June 2005 to 7 June 2006, the Company paid JPY8.830335mn in total to the Bank, comprising the difference between the fixed interest rate and the floating interest rate, as well as penalty interest payments due to delays. These payments were subject to the agreement in question.

Japanese Court Decision

After the Company had executed the interest-rate swap agreement with the Bank, it asserted that the Bank had breached its duty of explanation, had abused its superior bargaining position, and had inappropriately and unfairly solicited the agreement. Therefore, the Company claimed damages from the Bank in accordance with the relevant laws.

In Japan, sellers of financial instruments had a duty of explanation. The Japanese Act on Sales of Financial Instruments, Article 3(1) provides[3]:

> When a Financial Instruments Provider, etc. intends to carry out Sales, etc. of Financial Instruments on a regular basis, he/she shall *explain* the following matters as specified below (hereinafter referred to as 'Important Matters') to Customers at or before the time that the Sale of Financial Instruments are carried out. [Emphasis added].

Also, sophisticated institutions like banks had a duty of explanation under tort and vicarious liability in the Japanese Civil Code (Articles 415, 709, and 715).[4]

The court of first instance denied that the Bank had breached its responsibilities, including those with regard to tort liability, respecting the vicarious liability related to a breach of duty of explanation, and dismissed all claims by the Company.[5] However, the case was appealed, and the court of second instance recognized that there had been a breach of duty of explanation by the Bank, affirmed the Bank's tort liability, and partially admitted the Company's claims for the following reasons[6]:

(1) According to explanations given by the person in charge at the Bank, although there had been a likelihood that the conditions established under the corresponding agreement would not have resulted in a satisfactory outcome regarding the risk-hedge functions accompanying interest rate fluctuations expected by the customer, no explanations to such effect were given; and

(2) Remarkably insufficient explanations were given regarding matters that could have possibly affected the customer's judgment concerning the appropriateness of execution of the agreement.

---

[3] Japanese Act on Sales of Financial Instruments (Act No. 101 of 31 May 2000), Article 4, https://www.mofo.com/resources/insights/200702-japan-one-stop-financial-services-intermediary-business, accessed 23 December 2016.

[4] For the Japanese Civil Code (Act No. 89 of 27 April 1896), Articles 415, 709, and 715, http://www.moj.go.jp/content/000056024.pdf, accessed 8 September 2016.

[5] Supra note 1.

[6] *Ibid.*

An appeal was filed against the aforementioned decision. In contrast to the previous decision, the Supreme Court denied there was a tort liability related to a breach of duty of explanation, quashed the ruling of the court of second instance, issued its own judgment, and dismissed the Company's appeal.

This Japanese Supreme Court's decision was made on an appeal of the lower court's decision of 27 April 2011, that the "bank breached its duty of explanation." The Japanese Supreme Court thus settled the conflict between the judgment of the first instance and that of the second instance. The Supreme Court individually and specifically indicated, as the reason why a tort liability could not be recognized, that there had been no breach of the duty of explanation.[7]

Economic Analysis

The courts decisions described above were made without rendering any solid economic analysis. A detailed assessment of the financial issues associated with this case should have been presented to the court. In addition, an experienced and credible financial expert should have been consulted and asked to present key facts and figures about the case to the court. This would have helped those who were making decisions to understand the immense evidence that was available and to facilitate the process by which they accessed the information needed to arrive at a robust verdict.

Although such an economic analysis should have played a more prominent role in the process by which the court made a determination, it was not included in the decisions and, as such, was not available for public analysis. To this end, the author has prepared the following economic analysis for this case study so that it could be employed to assess the court's decision. For this analysis, the author used the M.D.A. model and the method which were commonly used for the studies on an interest-rate swap in general.[8]

---

[7] *Ibid.*

[8] See M. Moffett, A. Stonehill, and D. Eiteman (2014). *Fundamentals of Multinational Finance*, 5th edn. (New York: Addison-Wesley Publishing), pp. 370–373. (M.D.A stood for Moffett, Stonehill, and Eiteman).

(1) *Interest-Rate Swap*

A swap was a derivative instrument that involved a contractual agreement through which two parties exchanged the cash flow or economic performance of a specific financial asset. Typically, this might be the cash flow associated with interest payments on a debt generated from a variable rate, otherwise known as a floating rate loan. Party A might agree with Party B to exchange (swap) the floating rate for a fixed rate, and this was known as an *interest-rate swap*.[9] For a firm that had an existing debt obligation, the swap allowed the debtor to alter its cash-flow obligations. It had no effect on the outstanding capital owed to the creditor, but was rather an alteration of the cash flow associated with interest payments. Swapping fixed for floating interest rates fell into the category of financial derivatives, and was known as a *plain vanilla swap*, i.e., it was one of the simplest types of traded derivatives. As such, this type of swap trading represented the single largest financial derivative market in the world.[10]

Motivations for entering into such a trade could vary; however, the most common reason was the borrower's changing interest rate expectations. For example, a borrower that had a strong credit profile and outstanding floating-rate debt obligation might, after reviewing the prevailing market conditions, conclude that interest rates were about to rise. In order to avoid an anticipated increase in debt repayments, the company might decide to enter into a swap agreement with a counterparty to pay a fixed rate and receive a floating one. If interest rates rose as anticipated, the firm would continue to pay the same amount of interest on its debt, but would receive higher amounts from the other party. As the original debt obligation remained unchanged, the firm could be said to have changed its debt profile from floating to fixed. Table 1 summarily illustrates interest-rate swap strategies for companies that hold either fixed-rate or floating-rate debts.[11]

The cash flow associated with an interest-rate swap was calculated on a set amount of capital, which was referred to as the notional principal. This amount was agreed to between the two parties to the swap before a deal was finalized. The notional principal should be set to cover their interest rate management needed, but normally matched the company's

---

[9] *Ibid.*

[10] *Ibid.*

[11] *Ibid.*

Table 1: Strategies for Interest-Rate Swap

Current Position	Future Expectation	Strategy
Fixed-rate debt	Interest rates to rise to fall	No action
		Pay floating/Receive fixed
Floating-rate debt	Interest rates to rise to fall	Pay fixed/Receive floating
		No action

original loan in order to meet the interest payments. For that reason, interest-rate swaps were often also known as *coupon swaps*. Such swaps were a contractual agreement purely between a swap dealer and a company. The extent to which such derivatives would be used was entirely at the company's discretion.[12]

The interest-rate swap market existed because money markets were not perfectly efficient. If all companies had free and equal access to the world's capital markets, regardless of interest rate structures or currency differences, it was likely that the interest-rate swap market would not exist at all. In reality, interest-rate swaps were a flourishing market and provided benefits to all parties. Due to comparative cost savings, they were often described as representing a proverbial "free lunch" to those entities that had the best access to capital markets.[13]

(2) *Comparative Cost Savings*

This was because capital markets treated companies with different credit ratings differently. In this case, the Bank and the Company were both looking to borrow JPY300mn for a six-year period, and the Bank had a triple-A credit rating (the highest), while the Company was rated triple-B (the lowest investment-grade debt rating). It was likely that the Bank would have access to a wider range of fixed and floating-rate loans at cheaper rates than the Company. This was because a creditor would demand a higher interest rate from a lower-rated borrower to compensate for the increased risk of default. In this case, the Bank might decide to borrow at a fixed rate, as it already had a large stock of outstanding

---

[12] *Ibid.*

[13] D. Duffie and K.J. Singleton (1997). "An Econometric Model of the Term Structure of Interest-Rate Swap Yields," *The Journal of Finance*, 52(2), 1287–1321.

Figure 1: Swap Structure

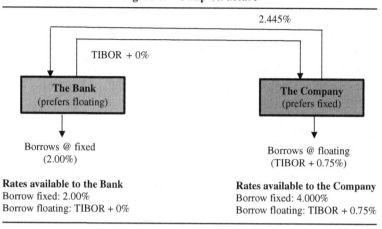

floating-rate loans. On the other hand, the Company would prefer to borrow at a fixed rate, but might have to pay a higher price for the loans due to its credit rating. Therefore, it might seek to borrow in a way in which it had a comparative cost savings, and then enter into a swap to exchange the floating rate for a fixed rate. This is illustrated in Figure 1.

(3) *Mechanics of the Swap*

If each party behaved perfectly rationally, they would both borrow in the market where they had a comparative cost savings. In this case, as demonstrated in Figure 1, the Bank was able to borrow fixed-rate funds at 2%, which was 2% cheaper than the Company, which must pay 4% for the same loan, could. For a floating-rate loan, however, the Bank could borrow funds at a rate that was 0.5% lower than the Company could: spread 0.25% compared to spread 0.75%.

Comparing 2% and 0.5%, the Bank's relative comparative cost saving is to borrow fixed-rate funds and so the Company should borrow floating-rate funds.

The steps the two parties undertook in Figure 1 were:

(1) The Bank was able to borrow at the fixed rate of 2.000% p.a. before entering into a six-year term through which it agreed to *receive a fixed pay floating* interest-rate swap with the Company.

(2) The agreement specified that the Bank would pay the Company a floating interest rate, a 3 month TIBOR + 0%. This allowed the Bank to repay the debt on a floating basis, as it preferred. The interest rate that the Bank negotiated with the Company might be lower than that at which the Company would have been able to borrow on its own.

(3) The Company was able to access a floating rate of 3 month TIBOR + 0.75%. Once this rate was secured, it agreed to *receive a floating pay fixed* interest-rate swap with the Bank for the life of the swap agreement, which in this case was six years.

(4) The Company agreed to pay a fixed rate of interest of 2.445% to the Bank. This enabled the Company to make the preferred fixed-rate debt service payments at a lower cost than it would have been able to acquire on its own.

(4) *Cost Savings Associated with Swap*

The following was the position of the two parties in this case:

	The Bank	The Company
Credit ratings as borrowers	AAA	BBB
Prefers to borrow	Floating	Fixed
Fixed-rate cost of borrowing	2.000%	4.000%
Floating-rate cost of borrowing:		
TIBOR (value is unimportant)	TIBOR	TIBOR
Spread	0.000%	0.7500%
Total floating-rate	(TIBOR)%	(TIBOR + 0.75)%

Here is the Bank's comparative borrowing cost saving:

	Values
Bank's absolute cost saving:	
in fixed-rate borrowing	2.000%
	(minus)
in floating-rate borrowing	0.75%
Comparative cost saving in fixed rate	1.250%

The question was how the Bank's 1.25% comparative cost savings could be distributed as savings to each party.

The Bank was able to borrow the funds at a fixed rate of 2.000%. Having done so, it entered into a swap agreement whereby it paid a floating rate of TIBOR + 0%. The Company had the following combined interest payments:

The Bank borrowed at fixed rates:	(2.000%)	
Swaps *fixed for floating rates*:	2.445%	Received fixed
	(TIBOR)	Paid floating
Net interest (debt + swap)	(TIBOR – 0.445%)	

The Company borrowed funds at a floating rate of interest: TIBOR + 0.75%. The swap agreement allowed it to swap a floating rate for fixed rate of interest. This meant that it would pay a 2.445% fixed rate of interest while receiving a floating rate of TIBOR + 0%.

The Company borrowed at floating rates:	(TIBOR + 0.75%)	
Swaps *floating for fixed rates*:	TIBOR + 0%	Received floating
	(2.445%)	Paid fixed
Net interest (debt + swap)	(3.195%)	

This scenario was beneficial for each of the borrowers because they were able to borrow at a preferred interest rate structure at a lower rate than they would have been capable of attaining on their own. But how can this be the case for cost savings for both parties?

	The Company	**The Bank**
If borrowing directly	(4%)	(TIBOR + 0%)
If borrowing through swap	(3.195)	(TIBOR – 0.445%)
Cost savings	+ 0.805%	+ 0.445%
Total cost savings	1.25 (= 0.805 + 0.445) %	

The 1.25% comparative cost savings enjoyed by Bank represented the opportunity for cost savings for both parties. This 1.25% was distributed as a 0.805% saving to the Company and a 0.445% saving to the Bank. Each party benefited because of the specialization of borrowing funds in their preferred market by subsequently exchanging interest payment streams for cost savings.

(5) *The Company's Position: Swapping for Fixed Rates*

The Company's management was concerned about its existing floating-rate loan. The Company had been led to believe that there was a strong possibility that interest rates, in particular TIBOR, would increase within the next three years (see Exhibit 2). However, because the loan was so recent, refinancing would have been too expensive. Therefore, the management was of the opinion that an interest-rate swap, through which they could pay a fixed rate of interest while receiving a floating interest rate, might be an effective means of fixing future interest rates. The Bank offered the Company a fixed rate of 2.445% against three months' TIBOR + 0%. By entering into the swap agreement, the Company would receive a TIBOR + 0% and pay 2.445% on a notional principal of JPY300mn over

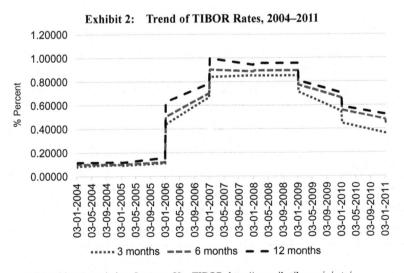

Exhibit 2:   Trend of TIBOR Rates, 2004–2011

Source: All Banking Association, Japanese Yen TIBOR, http://www.jbatibor.or.jp/rate/.

Table 2: **The Company's Interest-Rate Swap (Pay Fixed/Receive Floating) for 8 June 2005– 8 March 2006**

Interest Rates	Variability	8 June/05	8 September/05	8 December/05	8 March/06
TIBOR (floating)	Rise or fall	−0.08000	−0.08917	−0.09000%	−0.118180%
Spread (fixed)	Fixed	−0.75%	−0.75%	−0.75%	−0.75%
Total interest payable		−0.83000%	−0.83917%	−0.84000%	−0.86818%
Swap Interest Rates					
Pay fixed	Fixed	−2.445	−2.445%	−2.445%	−2.445%
Receive floating TIBOR		+0.08000%	+0.08917%	+0.09000%	+0.11818%
Combined Loan and Swap Position					
TIBOR on loan	Paying	−0.08000%	−0.08917%	−0.09000%	−0.11818%
Spread (fixed)	Paying	−0.75%	−0.75%	−0.75%	−0.75%
Pay fixed on swap	Paying	−2.445%	−2.445%	−2.445%	−2.445%
Receive floating TIBOR on swap		+0.08000%	+0.08917%	+0.09000%	+0.11818%
Net interest due after swap		**−3.195%**	**−3.195%**	**−3.195%**	**−3.195%**

the course of the next six years. Table 2 presents a quick overview of the combined existing loan and the "pay fixed/receive floating" swap.

It is important to note that this swap agreement was not intended to replace the existing loan but supplement it. The Company was still legally obliged to fulfill all the requirements of the floating rate loan agreement. The swap agreement also did not include the repayment of principal, but applied only to the loan interest payments. The portion of the debt service payment that the Company was concerned about, the benchmark TIBOR base rate, was directly offset by the receipt of the TIBOR cash flow from the Bank, the counterparty to the swap. The Company was only responsible for repaying the cash flow of the spread over this benchmark, i.e., +0.75%, plus the fixed payment of 2.445% to the Bank. Combining both rates resulted in a total fixed interest payment of 3.195% on the loan principal of JPY3mn, as illustrated in Table 2.

With the Company now making net fixed interest rate payments of 3.195%, it had protected itself from rising debt-servicing payments in the event that market interest rates rose. The floating rate interest payments received from the Bank on the other side of the swap were used to service the original debt interest obligations. So, on a net basis, the Company was now making fixed interest rate payments by means of the swap. Therefore, the Company had synthetically transformed a floating-rate loan into fixed-rate debt.

Given that lenders offered rates above 3.19% and assuming that the Company wished to lock in fixed rates for the remaining loan duration, it appeared that this swap trade represented a good deal for the Company. However, if the rates quoted to the Company were to fall below 3.19% in the future, the Company would suffer loss of the difference between 3.195% and the market rate quoted. As Exhibit 2 indicated, the market interest rates for the period during the transaction period from 8 March 2005 until 8 March 2011 remained below 3.19%. In fact, analyzing trade performance in hindsight or attempting to profit from changing interest rate expectations was pure speculation.[14] Nevertheless, as the motivation behind the trade was for the Company to hedge its interest rate risk and secure certainty about its cash flow, it must still be considered as a real possibility for hedging such risk.

(6) *Company Ends Swap*

As with any loan agreement or financial transaction, one of the parties to the swap might wish to terminate the transaction at some future date. This was possible if early termination rights had been agreed upon. In this case, the Company did terminate the swap agreement with the Bank. The original deal, which was struck on 4 March 2004, specified JPY300mn as the notional principal, fixed-rate interest payments of 2.445% p.a., and a floating rate of three-month TIBOR + 0% to be exchanged and paid on 8 June 2005, as the Company had opted for a swap agreement in which transactions would commence one year from the trade date, and on the eighth of every third month thereafter, from 8 March 2005 to 8 March 2011.

For the period from 8 June 2005 to 7 June 2006, the Company paid the Bank JPY8.830335mn, which represented the difference between the fixed interest rate and floating rate payments, plus the delayed penalty interest payment, as specified in the agreement.

---

[14]B.A. Minton (1997). "An Empirical Examination of Basic Valuation Models for Plain Vanilla U.S. Interest-Rate Swaps," *Journal of Financial Economics*, 44(2), 251–277.

Table 3: Timetable of Events

Contract Made	Swap Started	Interest Payment for One Year				Paid	Contract Ends
+	+					+	+
3/8, 04	3/8, 05	6/8, 05	9/8, 05	12/8, 05	3/8, 06	6/8, 06	3/8, 11

Table 4: Applicable TIBOR Rates

TIBOR (3 months)	8 June 2005	0.08000% p.a.
	8 September 2005	0.08917
	8 December 2005	0.09000
	8 March 2006	0.11818

Source: All Banking Association, Japanese Yen TIBOR, http://www.jbatibor. or.jp/rate/.

The timetable of events for the swap is detailed in Table 3.

Details of the payments of JPY8.830335mn by the Company for one year, from 8 June 2005 to 7 June 2006, were as follows:

The Company's payments on 8 June 2006 for one year at the time of termination of the swap were calculated as the difference between the fixed interest rate of 2.445% and the floating interest rates (three-month TIBOR) for one year for JPY300mn (see Table 4). For the following calculation, it should be noted that fixed 2.445% and three-month TIBOR were to be paid on a 1-year basis. Each interest payment was on a 4-month basis and so annual interest payments had to be divided by 3 for the 4-month payments.

$$[(0.02445 - 0.0008000)/3 + (0.02445 - 0.0008917)/3$$
$$+ (0.02445 - 0.0009000)/3 + (0.02445 - 0.0011818)/3]$$
$$\times \text{JPY300mn} = [0.0078833 + 0.0051776 + 0.00515$$
$$+ 0.007756] \times \text{JPY300mn} = 0.0259669$$
$$\times \text{JPY300mn} = \text{JPY7.79007mn}.$$

The termination penalty and delayed penalty interest payment were JPY1.040265mn. Total payment by the Company to the Bank was JPY8.830335mn.

The Company was unhappy with this payment and subsequently initiated legal action against the Bank, on 8 June 2006. The Company sued the Bank for damages of JPY8.830335mn on the basis that it believed the Bank had failed to adhere to its duty of explanation, had abused the fact that it was in a superior bargaining position, and had unfairly instigated the agreement with the Bank by means of an abusive transaction.

Court Decision in England

Mr. Miyashita, the Company's president, was aware that the interest-rate swap had originated in the London branch of the Bank, which had subsequently offered it through the Tokyo office. He therefore contemplated suing the Bank's London branch. He sought advice from the Company's legal advisor and researched what potential course of action might be available to the Company to sue the Bank in the UK. As Britain was a common-law jurisdiction, he hoped that the UK courts would handle the case differently than the Japanese courts, which were governed by statutory law. The Company's experiences with Japanese courts had been negative and he hoped he would get a better result elsewhere.

In response to this request, the legal advisor submitted the following report on the leading case on the same issue[15]:

> Since 2010, many different companies throughout the world had stood accused of misselling interest rate hedging products. It was worth comparing the Japanese court case that was described above, which was leveraged in a country that was ruled by civil and statutory law, with that of a British claim of interest-rate swap misselling, which was leveraged in a country that was governed by common law.
>
> In 2011, John Green and Paul Rowley (GR) bought a case against The Royal Bank of Scotland PLC (RBS).[16] In early 2005, Green and Rowley had agreed a swap contract with RBS as a means of protecting themselves against increases in interest rates on loans that had been taken to

---

[15]This is an internal document from the legal advisor to the president.

[16]UK, John Green & Paul Rowley v. Royal Bank of Scotland Plc (2012) EWHC3661, http://lexlaw.co.uk/wp-content/uploads/2012/12/GreenFinalJudgment.pdf, accessed 5 December 2016. The judgement was made on 21 December 2012, in the Manchester Mercantile Court by His Honor Judge Waksman QC.

support a property purchase. By May of the same year, the Claimants had come to the conclusion that the "rates would come down in the short term and then rise so were keen to hedge at current market rates." As such, they had developed their own view of how the interest rates would perform in the future, and this view was not necessarily supported by information from a third party. They subsequently made the decision to enter into a ten-year interest-rate swap as a means of protecting themselves against any future interest rate increases.

At the time the Claimants entered into this agreement, they had an existing loan from RBS that was valued at £1.5mn, to be repaid over a period of 15 years on an interest-only basis of 1.5% above the base rate. Before agreeing to the swap, the Claimants met with two representatives of RBS, who supplied information about the potential interest swap. The Claimants later signed a contract containing a swap agreement that consisted of a fixed base rate of 4.83% to be applied to a notional amount of £1.5mn. The swap operated in such a way that, if the interest rates were to fall below 4.83%, the amount of money the Claimants needed to repay on their loan would decrease, but they would also be required to pay RBS a corresponding sum under the swap. The Claimants benefited from the swap for a period of time, particularly between 2006 and 2007, when the interest rates increased. However, in March 2009, the interest rates plummeted to an all-time low, and they suffered under the agreement. In itself, the swap was relatively straightforward, and there was nothing particularly wrong with it; in essence, Green and Rowley had fallen victim to bad luck.

GR expressed an interest in restructuring their loan and the swap agreement. However, they were informed that they would be unable to do so without incurring a significant charge as a result of breaking the swap contract. In addition, they could not transfer the loans to a second bank without their having to pay a higher margin above the base rate because no other parties were prepared to accept the transfer with the swap in place. This issue was relatively common among parties that had agreed swap contracts and that subsequently wanted to refinance or restructure loans.

Finding themselves in an untenable situation, GR initiated legal action against RBS claiming damages; however, all their claims were dismissed. The Claimants had sued on the basis that they had been missold the swap and that RBS had made misleading statements about the product and how the process worked. They argued that RBS was under a duty to advise them on the correct action to take but had not done so or that they were given negligent advice. Specifically, the following complaints had been formally made by the end of the trial:

(1) RBS had negligently informed the Claimants that the costs they would incur if they broke the swap would be relatively low. In reality, they were large. In any event, the bank should have clearly informed the Claimants of the specific costs associated with breaking the swap.
(2) RBS had been negligent in its assertion that the swap fixed both the loan base rate and the margin above the base rate or, alternatively, had specified that the margin would be eternally fixed.
(3) Representatives from RBS had advised the Claimants to enter into the swap, which was negligent.

During the case, the judge highlighted that the Claimants were highly experienced, intelligent business professionals. He clearly respected and listened to the statements provided by the RBS witnesses and, on the whole, accepted the evidence they provided. He described one of the witnesses in the case as someone who was "honest, careful, and reliable with a clear understanding of how she structured her meetings when instruments such as the swap were explained to customers." As such, he accepted RBS's case that no representatives from the RBS had, at any time, offered advice on the potential amount of break costs. He also maintained that the information on break costs provided to the Claimants at the time of the contract was fair and sufficient. The judge noted that the Claimants had been free to request further details if they felt their knowledge or understanding was lacking. He ruled that the Claimants had entered into the agreement with full knowledge of the fact that the swap itself did not fix the margin.

An important element of this case was the ruling that RBS had not advised or, by its conduct, not assumed responsibility to advice or not made a recommendation on the swap. He concluded that no advisory relationship had been in existence and, as such, it was not necessary to pass any judgment on the effect of any "no advice" and "no reliance" provisions in the contract; however, he did raise the point that any "no advice" stipulations can be invoked to contradict or demarcate the extent of any duty of care.

Decision Time for the Company

In the summer of 2013, Mr. Miyashita, the Company's president, questioned the decision of the Japanese courts and argued against its viability. He questioned why the banks had not been held accountable for failing to act in the clients' best interest. Nor was he happy with the leading case in UK as provided above by his legal counselor.

Not all Company shareholders and directors were in agreement that the lawsuit was justified. Some major stakeholders questioned the action to sue the Bank following the court decision that the Bank had not breached its duty of explanation at the time the interest-rate swap was formally agreed to. This was made worse by the fact that the public had noticed the damages resulting from the use of the derivatives. However, Mr. Miyashita, the Company's president, stood by the decision to sue the Bank and argued that the stakeholders would appreciate the firm's transparency. He was also of the opinion that the lawsuit the Company instigated would serve as a warning sign to other companies that were considering entering into derivative contracts.

Mr. Miyashita faced a further dilemma: Should the Company continue to hedge by entering into interest-rate swaps, despite the fact that its previous agreements to do so had resulted in heavy losses? Participating in an interest-rate swap would mean the Company could not take advantage of the lower interest payments on offer when general interest rates fell. Hedging or un-hedging was really the issue for the Company. He fully understood now the economics and risks involved in the interest-rate swaps. However, failing to hedge was also not without risk and could impact the Company's access to alternative hedge options down the line.

The Company was in possession of a portfolio of negative and positive cash flows that were subject to the performance of interest rates. Mr. Miyashita was fully aware that effective financial risk management involved carefully managing the risks associated with interest rates. He also knew that many companies choose to remain unhedged on the premise that interest rate exposures were a common part of everyday business. Such businesses operated on the understanding that "interest rate netting," the netting of various interest rate payments and receivables, should work to reduce the risks of changes in interest rates. He still questioned whether stockholders wanted management to hedge against interest rate risk. He wondered if they might prefer to diversify and thereby lower risk through the ownership of other securities.

The experience had taught Mr. Miyashita that a company should not enter into hedging strategies without first defining expectations on interest rate movement. Having established these expectations, the company could then consider hedging, albeit while carefully evaluating the different strategies and techniques available. The president believed that those employing derivatives would need to be savvy enough to select the most effective hedging vehicle aligned with the Company's risk and return "utility" function. The Company's experiences with the Bank had taught the president that it was essential for corporate management personnel to be fully aware of the real risks and benefits associated with a financial instrument before employing it. In addition, once an agreement had been entered into, it was imperative that the performance of the hedge was continually monitored and the associated risks adequately managed.

Mr. Miyashita concluded that there was a need for middle-management offices consisting of risk management teams who were tasked with quantitatively monitoring derivative transactions in advance of trading, in order to ensure that all corporate policies and strategies were fully adhered to. He also believed there was a need for external investment advisors and appraisers to monitor the risks associated with derivatives.

For Further Discussion

(1) How important is it to present economic analysis during court cases that involve financial derivatives?

(2) What obligations does the Bank have to the customer? Present an evaluation of the decisions the court made.

(3) What are the pros and cons of interest-rate swaps?

(4) Suppose you were the president of the company that employed the interest-rate swap transaction in question to hedge against interest-rate risks. What is your opinion on the events that unfolded?

  (a) If you were presented with the same circumstances again, would you engage in the swap? Would you use it as a form of hedging or a form of speculation?

  (b) If you had entered into the swap, what should the Bank have explained to you before the contract was signed? Do you believe that the Bank breached its duty of explanation or abused its bargaining position? Do you think the swap agreement was unfair?

Case 4

Toyota's New Business Model: Creating a Sustainable Future*

No matter how severe the management environment becomes, or, rather, the more severe it becomes, the more we have to become a company that can steadily continue to grow, as a tree accumulates growth rings.[1]

— Akio Toyoda, President, Toyota Motor Corporation

Acknowledged as the world's leading automotive manufacturer, the Toyota Motor Corporation (see Exhibit 1) was one of the world's largest companies by revenue and had more than 369,000 employees globally.[2] Other manufacturers copied the company's philosophy and successful business model: the "Toyota Way"; its strategies were emulated worldwide as a recognized leader in business models.

---

*Professor Mitsuru Misawa prepared this case for class discussion. Dr. Misawa is a professor of finance and director of the Center for Japanese Global Investment and Finance at the University of Hawaii at Manoa. This case is not intended to show effective or ineffective handling of decision or business processes. The authors might have disguised certain information to protect confidentiality. Cases are written in the past tense, this is not meant to imply that all practices, organizations, people, places, or fact mentioned in the case no longer occur, exist, or apply.

[1]A. Toyoda, "Financial Results Press Conference — Session 2," Toyota, 8 May 2019, https://global.toyota/en/newsroom/corporate/27803157.html#speech, accessed 14 July 2019.

[2]"Overview: Toyota Motor Corporation," https://global.toyota/en/company/profile/overview/, accessed 18 July 2019.

Exhibit 1:   Company Profile — Toyota

Company Name	Toyota Motor Corporation
Main Business	Motor vehicle production and sales
President	Akio Toyoda
Date Established	August 28, 1937
Capital	$3,970.5 million (2018)
Annual Sales	$293.80 billion (2018)
Profits	$24.94 billion (2018)
Head Office	1 Toyota-Cho, Toyota City, Aichi Prefecture 471–8571, Japan
Number of Employees	369,124 (2018)[a]

Note: [a]"Overview," Toyota Motor Corporation, https://global.toyota/en/company/profile/overview/, accessed 22 July 2019.
Source: Toyota 2018 Annual Report, http://www.toyota-global.com/investors/ir_library/, accessed 22 July 2019.

Exhibit 2:   Profile — Akio Toyoda

Akio Toyoda is the grandson of Kiichiro Toyoda, the founder of Toyota Motor Corporation. The Japanese business executive and the current president of Toyota joined the company in 1984. He became CEO of the world's largest vehicle maker in 2009.

Unlike his predecessors, Akio studied overseas and received an MBA from Babson College in the US.

Source: Akio Toyoda, *Forbes*, https://www.forbes.com/profile/akio-toyoda/#377576e86d3d, accessed 22 July 2019.

Although he had been president of the corporation for less than a year, Akio Toyoda (see Exhibit 2) realized the company, headquartered in Aichi, Japan, faced a crisis. Only a few years earlier, the *Forbes* annual Global 2000 list had included the conglomerate in the top 10 listed companies worldwide.[3] But since then, its financial rating had fallen significantly, indicating the company faced serious challenges.

After a period of rapid expansion, Toyota's vehicle sales plummeted in the wake of the global financial crisis and showed no sign of recovery.[4]

---

[3]S. DeCarlo, "The Forbes Global 2000," *Forbes*, 31 March 2005, https://www.forbes.com/2005/03/30/05f2000land.html#3e7b538a2b95, accessed 22 July 2019.

[4]"Toyota Keeps Eye on Priorities as Earnings Face Turn for Worse," *Nikkei Asian Review*, 12 May 2016, https://asia.nikkei.com/NAR/Articles/Toyota-keeps-eye-on-priorities-as-earnings-face-turn-for-worse, accessed 8 October 2016.

Exhibit 3: Company Profile — Ina Food

Company Name	Ina Food Industry Co. Ltd.
Main Business	Production and sales of agar powder
Chairman and CEO	Hiroshi Tsukakoshi
President and COO	Osamu Inoue
Date Established	18 June 1958
Capital	$0.968 million (2018)
Annual Sales	$195.47 million (2018)
Operating Income	$17.14 million (2018)
Head Office	5074 Nishiharuchika, Ina-City, Nagano, Japan
Number of Employees	465 (2018)

Source: Ina Food Industry, 2018 Annual Report.

Additionally, the large-scale recall of various models, a process that started with those sold in the United States in 2009, had damaged the company's reputation.

Faced with these challenges, Toyoda wondered how the company could regain its earlier success and how to rebuild its reputation for quality mass production. He considered whether the Toyota Way could be modified or reinvented in a way that created sustainable business growth in the future.

He remembered a past conversation with the chairman of a traditional Japanese food manufacturer — the Ina Food Industry Company (Ina Food) (see Exhibit 3) — whose unique business philosophy had resulted in 55 years of continuous growth and profit (see Exhibit 4).

Such longevity intrigued Toyoda, and he wondered if he applied the same values to Toyota, the global company could return to sustainable, ongoing growth. Could such a large multinational company like Toyota gain new and powerful insights from such a small firm?

Discovering a New Path

Toyota's huge losses followed a period of rapid expansion, something Toyoda realized that Ina Food avoided with its management philosophy, known as the *Nenrin* approach to management.

Translated from Japanese, *Nenrin* meant "tree ring." While Ina Food's business model promoted annual growth, it also emphasized the virtue of

Exhibit 4:   Sales, Operating Income, and Employee Numbers for Ina Food, 1989–2018

INA FOOD INDUSTRY Co.,Ltd.

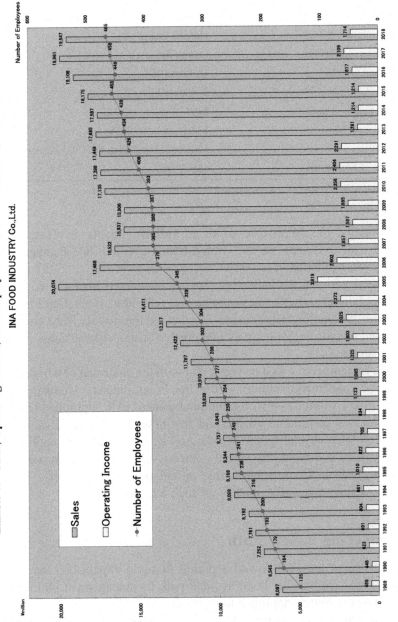

Source: Ina Food Industry, 2018 Annual Report.

slow and steady gains on an ongoing basis, much like the annual growth rings in the trunks of trees.

Ina Food was a small company based in the city of Ina in Nagano Prefecture, in the Japanese Alps. The firm's primary product was powdered agar, produced from seaweed. Widely used in Asian desserts and as a vegetarian substitute for gelatin, one popular use of agar in Japanese cuisine was *yōkan*, a jellied dessert made with red bean paste, agar, and sugar.

Aiko Toyota was deeply inspired when he heard Ina Food's chairman, Hiroshi Tsukakoshi, outline his Nenrin management strategy at a Toyota-related event. Unlike Toyota's business model at that time, Ina Food's philosophy strongly emphasized sustainability. The Nenrin strategy also indicated that growth slowed as a company moved from start-up to maturity. Tsukakoshi believed that the growth-ring approach also changed with time: "The size of [the] ring was big when young and getting small when grown. This was a natural rule, and companies should be like that too."[5]

Growing Through Sustainability

Let us build a good company. I hope to make it a company not just with good management indices, but a company that people would call a good company.[6]

— Hiroshi Tsukakoshi, Chairman, Ina Food

Tsukakoshi acknowledged that external events influenced the extent to which a company grew. However, he believed the most important factor was that an organization continued to grow at a steady pace without erratic expansion or contraction.

The Nenrin management approach also considered social, cultural, and economic dimensions.

It no longer measured success purely in terms of corporate earnings. Instead, it viewed the future of a business in terms of the extent to which it was sustainable, its broader influence on the people it served, and the environment within which it operated.

---

[5]H. Tsukakoshi (2005). *Iikaisha wo Tsukurimashou* [H. Tsukakoshi, *Let Us Build a Good Company*], 7th edn. (Nagano, Japan: Bunya Publishing Company), pp. 11–213.
[6]*Ibid.*

Toyoda believed that Ina Food's positive performance for more than half a century was a testament to the effectiveness of the Nenrin model of corporate sustainability. He decided to incorporate Tsukakoshi's approach into Toyota's existing model and hoped this would make the company more sustainable worldwide.

Steps to Positive Change

It was also a period in which our company, faced with quite a number of crises, was able to strengthen its sense of unity and my ability to unite. I keenly felt that rapid growth inconveniences many stakeholders if it is followed by a rapid fall.[7]

— Akio Toyoda, President, Toyota Motor Corporation

The Nenrin management approach incorporated four fundamental principles. These included the following:

- long-term strategic thinking,
- employee satisfaction,
- connecting with customers,
- community contribution.

Toyoda recognized that Tsukakoshi viewed short-term thinking as the application of analytical skills within established subject areas, while long-term thinking involved identifying the obstacles that impeded the development of sound critical thinking and action to overcome such obstacles. For example, businesses that used short-term thinking tended to establish unreasonably high sales targets. Although profits increased in the short term, this strategy posed an obstacle in planning for profits in the long term. In an effort to access short-term returns on investments, many shareholders pushed companies to increase profits in the short to medium term. However, the Nenrin approach viewed such action as having the potential to undermine the long-term prospects of a company, a move that conceivably had a negative impact on shareholder returns.

This belief underpinned the Ina Food philosophy. It was derived from Tsukakoshi's belief that "[t]hose who planned for the distant future would

---

[7] *Ibid.*

be rich and those who planned for the near future would be poor,"[8] a philosophy inspired by Ninomiya Sontoku (1787–1856),[9] a prominent Japanese philosopher, moralist, and economist, highly respected in Japan for his work on ethics and benevolence.

Shareholders added an additional burden on a business as they sought short-term returns on investments. In order to meet their expectations, management often went to great lengths to establish avenues of short-term growth, e.g., through increased prices, production capacity, or output efficiency.

Ina Food also faced a period of unexpected demand for its products, but unlike the Toyota Motor Group, which scaled up production to meet demand, Tsukakoshi resisted the temptation to increase profits. Instead, the chairman of Ina Food decided on a very different approach.

When Ina Food experienced an unexpected spike in demand for its products, Tsukakoshi recognized that the company's future rate of production could not be maintained. He decided not to increase production to meet increased demand. He also limited distribution to current customers on a proportional basis. He reasoned that demand would diminish once the media interest, which created the spike, was forgotten and the hype died down. He was correct in this assumption. Demand returned to normal levels, and some distributors even asked if they could return unsold products.

Akio Toyoda decided that Toyota's management should also adopt a similar approach. In a conversation with Tsukakoshi, he agreed that although profit was important, he wanted to see steady growth over a longer term. "We have to grow even under adverse wind like our recall crisis in 2009. Continuous growth is a key; and balancing the pace of speed is mandatory for that."[10,11]

---

[8] *Ibid.*

[9] Sontoku, Ninomiya (1983). *Kodansha Encyclopaedia of Japan*, Vol. 6 (Tokyo: Kodansha), pp. 7–8.

[10] S. Evans and A. MacKenzie, "The Toyota Recall Crisis," *Modern Trend*, 27 January 2010, https://www.motortrend.com/news/toyota-recall-crisis/, accessed 22 July 2019.

[11] H. Tsukakoshi and A. Toyoda, "Eienni Owarinonai Kigyou — Nenrin Keiei" [H. Tsukakoshi and A. Toyoda (2015). "Sustainable Company — Nenrin Management"], *PHP* 21(1-2), 3–27.

Employee Satisfaction

> *A company exists for its employees. Happiness and steady growth make it possible for the company to grow forever.*[12]

> — Hiroshi Tsukakoshi, Chairman, Ina Food

The concept of permanent employment was treated very seriously in Japan. Companies were expected to be responsible for their employees and to ensure that they remained in gainful employment from the moment they were recruited to the mandatory retirement age of 60.[13]

Tsukakoshi believed a management focus on steady growth, as opposed to one focused on revenue, ensured that all company stakeholders, both internal and external, worked harmoniously together. He believed that a firm didn't exist simply for management or for its own benefit; it was there to serve the employees first. His philosophy also went beyond Ina Food's employees. He also believed the firm existed to serve society and its community.

A traditional Japanese belief in lifelong employment required Ina Food to invest in the development of its employees' skills. He ensured that his employees were satisfied with their jobs, which helped foster loyalty and that everyone worked toward a common goal. Tsukakoshi believed this approach resulted in a higher-quality product, reduced production costs, and enhanced its long-term corporate sustainability. As an employer, he operated a strict seniority-based promotion system.[14]

He stated that when employees were happy, morale increased and the organization made a positive contribution to society, although the ultimate reason for a viable firm was its own existence.[15]

---

[12] Supra note 5.

[13] "Japan: Supreme Court rules on Mandatory Retirement," Ogletree Deakins, 4 June 2019, https://ogletree.com/international-employment-update/articles/june-2019/japan/2019-06-04/japan-supreme-court-rules-on-mandatory-retirement/, accessed 22 July 2019.

[14] M. Misawa (2006). "Ina Food Industry: A New Management Philosophy for Japanese Businesses," Asian Case Research Centre, The University of Hong Kong, Ref. 06/305C, MT, pp. 1–13 and TN, pp. 1–7.

[15] Supra note 5.

With this philosophy in mind, Toyoda established a Toyota corporate motto for employees so that when they retired, they recalled their past career with these words: "My life at Toyota was happy."[16]

Connecting with Customers

Companies promoted their products and services or communicated with customers in numerous ways. Japanese companies communicated very differently than their Western counterparts. Those who worked in Japanese businesses tended to favor implied messages as opposed to direct expressions. Hence, Japanese companies did not invest significantly in the development of strategic communications plans.

This method of communication was culturally acceptable in Japan. As 99% of Japan's population was Japanese nationals, people shared similar views about what represented a commonsense approach. This homogeneity was reflected in the Japanese notion of *aun no kokyu* (being in unison) and *kuuki wo yomu* (the ability to "read the air"). Many Japanese businesses believed that employees intrinsically understood each other, and this negated the need to engage in explicit communication.

However, with the growing use of digital technology, Japanese firms needed to invest more heavily in communications strategies. They started to adopt tools similar to those used by Western companies to connect with customers, e.g., blogs, websites, and social media platforms. In Ina Food's case, Tsukakoshi believed that such personalized communications with customers proved more effective than electronic means, especially if a product was perceived to be a luxury or prestige brand.

He also recognized that technological advances meant consumers had more choices than ever, in terms of where they shopped and the channels they used to purchase goods. He perceived that a rapid shift in social values and in the business landscape, characterized by a lack of trust, meant the notion that people intrinsically understood one another no longer held true. He believed that business leaders needed to proactively engage with their customers, and he felt the most effective way this could be achieved was through personalized contact, based on a face-to-face model.

---

[16] Supra note 11.

Instead of a reliance on electronic communications, he created situations where customers and service representatives met in a shared space.

One example of the face-to-face model in action was the chairman's decision to open restaurants on the company's grounds. This gave customers a chance to experience its products and meet directly with representatives from the company. Even the name of Ina Food's product, Kanten Papa (Agar Father), was designed to appeal to customers and generated a sense of comfort. Another example of this personalized approach was that staff within the company's mail-order department answered client requests with handwritten letters.

Strategies like this helped transform customers from buyers to fans of the company and established a loyal base of repeat customers who kept buying, even when prices increased.

Toyoda agreed with Ina Food's approach and attempted to replicate Ina Food's example in his own practices. "I use 'Morizo' as my nickname and print it on my business card.[17] When I give it to our customers at our first meeting, they smile. This is important for our business, since they would be a Morizo fan,"[18] he stated. In Japanese culture, smiling was seen to be contagious, given its ability to emotionally connect people. It was regarded as one of the simplest yet most powerful expressions in traditional Japanese culture. The nickname originated from Japan's Expo 2005, which was held in Aichi Prefecture, Japan, where Toyota's headquarters was located. One of the expo's fluffy green mascots was called Morizo. People smiled when they saw Toyoda's nickname Morizo because they remembered the expo's iconic hairy green mascot.[19]

Community Contribution

Tsukakoshi also believed firms needed to practice corporate social responsibility. Businesses conducted in a sustainable manner protected the long-term future of an organization. It also served as an effective marketing tool that helped secure a firm's competitive advantage in a rapidly changing landscape. To this end, Ina Food established a spectacular 24-acre

---

[17] *Ibid.*

[18] Supra note 11.

[19] Expo 2005 Aichi Japan, "Official Mascots," http://www.expo2005.or.jp/en/whatexpo/mascot.html, accessed 17 September 2019.

garden that surrounded its factory. The local community, and the company's employees who tended the garden on a voluntary basis, enjoyed this park.

Connecting with the community also resonated with Toyoda. In a move that fostered global community support, he introduced the e-Toyota and GAZOO[20] projects. These schemes created a direct connection to the community Toyota served.

Toyoda stated that the e-Toyota business, which began with "e" for evolutionary, was, as its name implied, the vanguard business of Toyota's evolution and a banner for establishing next-generation business models that included intelligent vehicles. For cars, innovation in electronics meant increased value through enhanced safety, comfort, and environmental considerations.

The ongoing development of emerging markets and the rapid evolution of technology focused on sustainability and consumer needs meant the global economy was in a continual state of flux. Technology-driven change needed to be at the heart of any organization's interactions with consumers. It changed consumer behavior, the way in which partnerships were developed and sustained, and even a company's operational focus.[21]

Embracing Change

We were like a tree that grew too rapidly, that as a result was not able to form a strong enough trunk to protect it from the elements. Our fall into the red during the global financial crisis and our large-scale recalls were perhaps a result of this. I believe that sustainable growth means growing steadily each year under any circumstances.[22]

— Akio Toyoda, President, Toyota Motor Corporation

---

[20]Toyota, "e-Toyota & GAZOO, 75 Years of TOYOTA," November 2012, https://www.toyota-global.com/company/history_of_toyota/75years/message/index.html, accessed 3 September 2019.
[21]"White Paper: Digital Transformation of Industries Automotive Industry," World Economic Forum, January 2016, https://www.accenture.com/_acnmedia/accenture/conversion-assets/wef/pdf/accenture-automotive-industry.pdf, accessed 3 September 2019.
[22]Supra note 11.

Toyoda acknowledged he'd adopted Nenrin management principles when he announced Toyota's 2014 financial year results. Even five years later, when he presented the global manufacturer's latest financial results, he stated Toyota's success owed much to Tsukakoshi's philosophy.[23]

In a statement headlined "Aiming to Achieve Sustainable Growth and to Bring Smiles,"[24] Toyoda described how the vehicle manufacturer encountered numerous challenges between 2009 and 2014. He credited the tireless efforts of employees and the development of positive management practices and culture as having helped the corporation to meet those challenges. He believed that Toyota had undertaken positive steps toward sustainable growth and used the analogy of tree rings to highlight how Toyota's ongoing growth was dependent on the firm's ability to grow and develop in adversity.

In 2013, Toyota achieved the unprecedented milestone of reaching the sale of 10 million vehicles.[25] Despite the record production, Toyoda stressed that it was important that the company practiced self-restraint and avoided overextension. He believed the company needed to balance investments and direct management resources to areas that offered the most potential for sustainable growth.

He outlined how Toyota planned to pursue bold and innovative strategies in the future and make aggressive, forward-looking investments, such as its move to mobility services and collaborations, e.g., with ride-hailing platform Didi Chuxing.[26]

Toyoda stressed how the company's experience taught him that the group would only survive on a long-term basis if it designed and manufactured vehicles that excited customers. His goal was to ensure that Toyota evolved into a company that was capable of sustainable growth and that, even if faced with a crisis, the firm remained resilient and survived periods of adversity.

---

[23] *Ibid.*

[24] A. Toyoda, "Financial Results for Fiscal Year Ended March 2014," Toyota Motor Corporation, 8 May 2014, www.toyota-global.com, accessed 22 August 2019.

[25] Y. Takahashi, "Toyota Outputs Sets Industry Record," *Wall Street Journal*, 29 January 2014, https://www.wsj.com/articles/toyota-output-sets-industry-record-1390986041, accessed 22 July 2019.

[26] "Toyota Expands Collaboration in Mobility as a Service (MaaS) with Didi Chuxing, a Leading Ride-Hailing Platform," Toyota, 25 July 2019, https://global.toyota/en/newsroom/corporate/28993116.html, accessed 26 July 2019.

Valuable Lessons

The power of a long-term strategy that focused on gradual growth was highlighted in the example of the Nenrin management approach that fueled Ina Food's 55 years of continuous revenue and expansion. At a press conference in 2019 when the end-of-year financial results were announced, President Akio Toyoda remarked that through studying the actions of Ina Food, Toyota learned valuable lessons that helped the vehicle manufacturer to revise its operational and management strategies.[27]

Toyoda admitted that the multinational company's experience demonstrated that there was real potential for a new wave of strategic management knowledge and understanding to be gained from within successful small companies.[28] In 2019, when Toyoda reflected on the company's progress to date, he admitted the firm had been through a very difficult period.

The two company heads forged a strong relationship and met on an ongoing basis. In fact, Akio Toyota continued to be so inspired by the concept of Nenrin management that he referred to it in his speeches, presentations, and annual reports.[29]

Moving Forward

I keenly felt that rapid growth inconveniences many stakeholders if it is followed by a rapid fall. No matter how severe the management environment becomes, or, rather, the more severe it becomes the more we have to become a company that can steadily continue to grow, like how a tree accumulates growth rings (Nenrin management).[30]

— Akio Toyoda, President, Toyota Motor Corporation

---

[27] A. Toyoda, "Financial Results Press Conference — Session 2," Toyota, 8 May 2019, https://global.toyota/en/newsroom/corporate/27803157.html#speech, accessed 14 July 2019.
[28] Supra note 11.
[29] Y. Kubota, "To Whom Do Japan's Most Powerful Turn to for Advice? The Sensei of Seaweed," *Wall Street Journal*, 1 September 2015, https://www.wsj.com/articles/to-whom-do-japans-most-powerful-turn-for-advice-the-sensei-of-seaweed-1441069219, accessed 22 July 2019.
[30] A. Toyoda, "Financial Results Press Conference — Session 2," Toyota, 8 May 2019, https://www.youtube.com/channel/UC-XFpnxDaYpDdXYM57hk-VQ, accessed 3 September 2019.

The environment in which Toyota operated demanded change. Inspired by traditional Japanese philosophy, the company successfully turned around its business model when it adopted the slow and steady Nenrin approach.

Toyota's sales fell sharply during the global financial crisis of 2008–2009, and the manufacturer was also affected by large-scale recalls. However, sales have since recovered. In 2018, despite record production, Toyoda stressed that the company practiced the Nenrin approach of self-restraint and avoided overextension.

Toyota Motor Corporation Vehicle Sales (thousands of units)[31]

2008	2009	2010	2011	2012	2013	2014	2015	2016	2017	2018
8,913	7,567	7,237	7,308	7,352	8,871	9,116	8,972	8,681	8,971	8,964

Increased industrialization, together with the rapid evolution of technology, created environmental problems with a global impact. Many organizations directly contributed to environmental degradation, while the actions of many industries undermined peoples' health and added to global climate change[32] issues. When Toyota moved to address its business issues, it also looked to the future and the impact its vehicles had on the environment.

The automotive industry was revolutionized by digitalization, which led to the introduction of new business models focused on automation. Four specific disruptive technology-driven changes observed in the automotive sector included connectivity, diverse mobility, electrification, and autonomous driving.[33]

Toyoda was appointed head of the company's electric car division in 2016,[34] a move that reflected the company's commitment to electric

---

[31] Toyota Motor Corporation, 2018 Annual Report, https://global.toyota/en/ir/library/annual/, accessed 15 September 2019.

[32] "Environmental & Global Sustainability Issues," Environmental Professionals Network, EPN, 15 August 2014, http://environmentalprofessionalsnetwork.com/environmental-global-sustainability-issues/, accessed 30 July 2019.

[33] P. Gao, H.W. Kaas, D. Mohr, and D. Wee (January 2016). "Disruptive trends that will transform the auto industry," McKinsey & Company. https://www.mckinsey.com/industries/automotive-and-assembly/our-insights/disruptive-trends-that-willtransform-the-auto-industry, accessed 30 July 2019.

[34] M. Kudo, "Chief thirsts to identify 'real Toyota,'" *Nikkei Asian Review*, 17 November 2017, https://asia.nikkei.com/Business/Chief-thirsts-to-identify-real-Toyota, accessed 30 July 2019.

vehicles, its efforts to remain a key player in the automobile industry, and its determination to reduce its environmental impact. Although Toyota's first all-electric model had yet to be unveiled, it embraced a future where electric-powered vehicles reigned supreme.

Vehicles were once powered by fossil fuel, but newer battery-powered vehicles could run purely on electricity.[35] At the moment, electric cars represented a mere fraction of the global automobile market, which remained dominated by fossil fuel-powered entities. However, as the market for electric vehicles increased, the industry had undergone massive transformation. This change was supported by government schemes, particularly in China and Europe, which were designed to encourage people to buy electric vehicles, to improve air quality in cities, and to tackle pollution.[36]

In 2019, Toyota announced that it planned to focus on electric vehicles and to collaborate with battery makers in order to ensure the security of supply for future electric models.[37] However, its electrification strategies were heavily centered on hybrid vehicles, as opposed to battery-powered versions.

The vehicle manufacturer revealed that, by 2025 (five years ahead of previous estimates), half of its global sales would be electrified models.[38] Toyoda also said the industry was undergoing a "profound transformation," the extent of which only emerged every century.[39]

He believed significant efforts were needed to encourage consumer demand for vehicles that were powered by electric sources since less than

---

[35] C. Domonoske, "As More Electric Cars Arrive, What's the Future for Gas-Powered Engines?," National Public Radio, 16 February 2019, https://www.npr.org/2019/02/16/694303169/as-more-electric-cars-arrive-whats-the-future-for-gas-powered-engines, accessed 3 August 2019.

[36] "As More Electric Cars Arrive, What's the Future for Gas-Powered Engines?," *CPR News*, 16 February 2019, https://www.cpr.org/2019/02/16/as-more-electric-cars-arrive-whats-the-future-for-gas-powered-engines/, accessed 30 July 2019.

[37] F. Lambert, "Toyota Unveils Images of Upcoming All-Electric Cars, Accelerates EV Plans by 5 Years," *Electrek*, 7 June 2019, https://electrek.co/2019/06/07/toyota-electric-car-images-accelerate-plan/, accessed 3 August 2019.

[38] *Ibid.*

[39] C. Riley, "Toyota Sets Aggressive New Target for Electrified Cars," *CNN Business*, 7 June 2019, https://edition.cnn.com/2019/06/07/business/toyota-electric-cars/index.html, accessed 3 August 2019.

1% of all vehicles on the market were battery-powered.[40] He also stressed that car manufacturers needed to invest in solid-state battery technology to develop batteries that were lighter, more compact, and affordable.[41]

The question that remained for Toyota concerned how to maintain its industry-leading position in an environment that was characterized by challenges and uncertainty.

To this end, Toyoda focused his efforts on collaboration, and mergers and acquisitions. In 2019, Toyota announced that it had developed a new chassis specifically designed for electric cars in collaboration with Japanese carmaker Subaru.[42]

In the same year, Toyota and another Japanese vehicle manufacturer, Suzuki, announced that the two companies had entered into an alliance that established a long-term partnership in order to collaborate in new fields, i.e., autonomous driving.[43] Toyota's collaborations related to electric vehicles were not limited to only these companies. It also collaborated with different industries in order to develop the electric vehicle market.

The Toyota Motor Corporation, founded by Kiichiro Toyoda in 1937, is a multinational automotive manufacturer, headquartered in Japan.

In March 2018, its annual revenue was $294 billion. As of February 2018, it was the 13th largest company in the world by revenue.

Toyota was the largest automobile manufacturer in 2018 (by production) ahead of the Volkswagen Group and General Motors. The company was the first automobile manufacturer in the world to produce more than 10 million vehicles per year. It is a global market leader in sales of hybrid electric vehicles and also one of the largest companies to encourage the mass adoption of hybrid vehicles worldwide.

The Ina Food Company was established in 1958 to produce agar, a natural gelatin.

---

[40] "President Akio Toyota's Speech at CES 2018," Toyota, 9 January 2018, https://global. toyota/en/newsroom/corporate/20566886.html, accessed 3 August 2019.

[41] *Ibid.*

[42] Y. Omoro, "In Toyota and Suzuki Alliance, Two Families Find Common Ground," *Nikkei Asian Review*, 29 August 2019, https://asia.nikkei.com/Business/Automobile/In-Toyota-and-Suzuki-alliance-two-families-find-common-ground, accessed 3 September 2019.

[43] "Toyota and Suzuki Enter into Capital Alliance Agreement," Toyota Motor Corporation and Suzuki Motor Corporation, 28 August 2019, https://global.toyota/en/newsroom/ corporate/29375884.html, accessed 3 September 2019.

Ina Food developed sources from which the raw material could be imported and stored throughout the year. Through consolidation of production, the company created a highly efficient process, together with strong customer demand and a stable market that eliminated fluctuating prices.

For Further Discussion

(1) What is corporate sustainability? And why is it so important for contemporary organizations?
(2) Evaluate and explore the steps involved in developing a sustainable corporate strategy.
(3) Explore methods by which the sustainability of companies can be evaluated.
(4) Evaluate the differences between corporate social responsibility (CSR) and corporate sustainability (CS).

Case 5

Negative Interest Rates: The Bank of Japan Experience[*]

For more than 20 years, all efforts by the Japanese government and the Bank of Japan (BOJ) to revitalize the nation's economy failed to stop both its deflationary spiral and weak growth. To address these twin issues, Japanese Prime Minister Shinzo Abe unveiled a new fiscal strategy, known as "Abenomics," after he took office in 2012. His initiative aimed to end Japan's economic stagnation, boost domestic demand, increase gross domestic product (GDP) growth, and hold inflation at 2%.

Early in 2013, the central bank applied quantitative monetary easing (QE)[1] by buying Japanese government bonds (JGBs) with the aim of achieving an inflation target of 2% in two years. At that time, the short-term prime interest rate sat at 1.475% per year.

Although the BOJ's initial round of QE doubled its balance sheet in 2013, the question remained as to whether the new policy would be able to drive Japan's economy out of its stagnation.

---

[*]Professor Mitsuru Misawa prepared this case for class discussion. Dr. Misawa is a professor of finance and director of the Center for Japanese Global Investment and Finance at the University of Hawaii at Manoa. This case is not intended to show effective or ineffective handling of decision or business processes. The authors might have disguised certain information to protect confidentiality. Cases are written in the past tense, this is not meant to imply that all practices, organizations, people, places or fact mentioned in the case no longer occur, exist or apply.

[1]Bank of Japan (3 February 2016). "Introduction of Quantitative and Qualitative Monetary Easing with a Negative Interest Rate," https://www.boj.or.jp/en/announcements/release_2016/k160129a.pdf, accessed 20 November 2019.

In 2014, the government increased Japan's consumption tax from 5% to 8% to pay for social welfare spending, and in response, consumers reduced their personal spending while markets remained in turmoil. To relieve recessionary pressure, the central bank was forced to progress to a second, open-ended phase of quantitative and qualitative easing (QQE) that committed to annual asset purchases of JPY80tn (USD660bn), a strategy it hoped to continue until the 2% target inflation rate was achieved.[2] This too failed to achieve the desired results.

On 20 January 2016, Haruhiko Kuroda, the governor of the BOJ, and the central bank's policy board gathered in Tokyo, where they announced a radical plan — the introduction of QQE with a negative interest rate — to achieve inflation of 2% in the shortest time.

An experienced leader and former president of the Asian Development Bank, Kuroda was the bank's 31st governor. Kuroda's academic background at both the University of Oxford and the University of Tokyo had exposed him to Western fiscal policy. His bold strategy was unveiled halfway through his first five-year tenure with the central bank.

Kuroda's plan aimed to enhance lending and investment, and it also supported Abenomic policies. The BOJ's adoption of negative interest rates followed that of a handful of other central banks, which included the European Central Bank (ECB), and those of Denmark, Sweden, and Switzerland, that also implemented negative interest rates. Could Kuroda's policy gamble achieve its goal and hold inflation? What happened if it failed?

A Radical Step

Almost the entire rich world is stuck in a zero-interest-rate liquidity trap situation, and I think everybody is haunted by the possibility that there's no way out of it. If Japan shows a way out of that, it will be very encouraging.

— Greg Ip, *Wall Street Journal*[3]

---

[2]Bank of Japan (31 October 2014). "Expansion of the Quantitative and Qualitative Monetary Easing," https://www.boj.or.jp/en/mopo/mpmdeci/mpr_2014/k141031a.pdf, accessed 5 May 2020.

[3]J. McBride and B. Xu (15 February 2016). "Abenomics and the Japanese Economy," Council on Foreign Relations, https://www.cfr.org/backgrounder/abenomics-and-japanese-economy accessed 3 March 2020.

After Kuroda's announcement, the BOJ pursued monetary easing in three significant dimensions of the economy: interest rates, quantitative monetary policy, and qualitative monetary policies.[4]

As the central bank controlled Japan's money supply, the conventional way to stimulate the economy was to buy and sell government debt in small quantities as short-term JGBs. When the BOJ acquired JGBs in large amounts, the move was regarded as an unconventional policy. It was termed unconventional because by Japanese law, the BOJ was not allowed to purchase newly issued short-term government securities[5] as this was defined as "self-financing." The BOJ's purchase of short-term government securities was legal only for a limited amount of purchases under extreme circumstances. It was regarded as unconventional because it was undertaken in order to increase the money supply to the markets, which in this case was the aim of the central bank's move.

The bank also purchased longer-maturity government bonds, exchange-traded funds (ETFs), and Japan real estate investment trusts (J-REITs) to increase the money supply. These securities were qualitatively different, and this monetary policy formed the basis of qualitative easing.

The BOJ believed both monetary policies — quantitative and qualitative — needed to work together to create monetary easing.

Negative Territory

On 16 February 2016, a negative interest rate of –0.1% was added to all current accounts that financial institutions held with the central bank. Financial institutions that deposited money with the BOJ after this date lost money. This BOJ strategy encouraged financial institutions to lend their excess liquidity to industry rather than stash it away as a deposit.

In reality, with each current account that financial institutions held in the central bank, the BOJ created three tiers of interest, so that their deposit was then divided into three sections. The first tranche was paid

---

[4]H. Kuroda (7 March 2016). "Answers to Frequently Asked Questions on Quantitative and Qualitative Monetary Easing (QQE) with Negative Interest Rates," https://www.boj.or.jp/en/announcements/press/koen_2016/ko160307a.htm, accessed 2 March 2020.

[5]Bank of Japan Act, Law number: Act No. 67 of 1942, Japan, https://www.cas.go.jp/jp/seisaku/hourei/data/boja.pdf, accessed 21 July 2023.

interest (positive), the second was charged at the –0.1% negative interest rate, and the last third received zero interest rates. This method ensured that the implementation of negative interest rates did not substantially reduce the earnings of financial institutions and undermine their functions as financial intermediaries.

For example, if a financial institution deposited a hypothetical JPY90mn with the BOJ, the BOJ paid 0.1% interest on the first part of that deposit, JPY30mn. For the second tier, the central bank deducted 0.1% interest, and for the third tier of JPY30mn, the BOJ paid no interest.

Academically, a negative interest rate policy was an unusual monetary policy tool where nominal target interest rates were set with a negative value, below the theoretical lower bound of 0%.[6] In a practical sense, in adverse situations, depositors paid interest to banks.

Negative interest rates were used when increased spending and investment were needed. The policy was regarded as unorthodox, since those who held deposits were encouraged to spend rather than hold cash in banks where it incurred a guaranteed loss.[7] In effect, central banks penalized financial institutions for holding cash, in the hope that these penalties prompted institutions to increase lending.[8] In Japan's case, the central bank used negative rates in an attempt to boost economic growth because other incentives failed.

Abenomics in Action

As a direct result of Abenomics, Japan's economy exhibited signs of moderate recovery.[9] In the third quarter of 2016, Japan's growth accelerated. GDP increased by 2.2% in annualized terms, in the three months through to September. This move was significant because GDP had grown at less

---

[6]B. Beers and G. Scott (29 January 2020). "Negative Interest Rates Definition," *Investopedia*, https://www.investopedia.com/terms/n/negative-interest-rate.asp, accessed 3 March 2020.

[7]*Ibid.*

[8]"How Does a Negative Policy Rate Work?," *Japan Times*, 14 August 2019, https://www.japantimes.co.jp/news/2019/08/14/business/negative-rate-policy-work/#.XiPCARMzZjs, accessed 3 March 2020.

[9]J. Soble, "Why Japan's Economy Posted Surprisingly Strong Growth," *New York Times*, 13 November 2016, https://www.nytimes.com/2016/11/15/business/japan-economy-growth-trade.html, accessed 28 February 2020.

than 1% for the past two decades. But the nation's inflation rate remained at 1%, lower than the targeted rate of 2%, and deflation continued.

Inflation gradually increased, and income to spending rose across both household and corporate sectors. However, global risks continued.

Volatility in the global financial markets, caused by a fall in crude oil prices, and uncertainty surrounding emerging markets and commodity-export-led economies, especially that of China, eroded corporate confidence that Japan's economic recovery plan would work. Kuroda knew that if this happened, it undermined the positive inflation trends that had started to emerge.

To prevent this risk, and to ensure the price stability target of 2% was achieved, Kuroda's previous QQE strategy with a negative interest rate aimed to reduce the short end of the yield curve. In order to do this, negative interest rates applied to deposits held in current accounts caused a downward pressure on the interest rates across the full yield curve. The bank also increased the purchases of JGBs.

Kuroda hoped that combining QQE with a negative interest rate policy would help the bank gain more control of money market operations. Another key objective was to increase the BOJ's monetary base by at least JPY80tn (USD678bn) through the purchase of JGBs per year.[10] In 2016 when QQE with a negative interest rate was introduced, the outstanding balance of JGBs held by the BOJ was JPY400tn, or 40% of the total outstanding JGBs issued. In April 2013 when the QQE monetary policy was adopted by the BOJ, the outstanding balance was JPY130tn.

With the overall aim of reduced interest rates across the full yield curve, the BOJ operated a flexible purchase process that was aligned with financial market conditions. The remaining maturity of JGBs purchased by the government averaged between 7 and 12 years. The BOJ also purchased ETFs and J-REITs, at an annual rate of approximately JPY3tn and USD90bn, respectively. It also purchased commercial papers (an unsecured form of promissory notes) and corporate bonds at an annual rate of approximately JPY2.2tn and JPY3.2tn, respectively.

---

[10]"Financial Statements," Bank of Japan, https://www.boj.or.jp/about/account/index.htm/, accessed 5 May 2020.

Unchartered Waters

Although QE doubled the BOJ's balance sheet in 2013, inflation stagnated below 1%. The central bank then progressed to a second, open-ended phase of QQE that consisted of JPY80tn (USD678bn) in annual asset purchases.[11] In September 2014, total assets outstanding on the BOJ's balance sheet were JPY278tn (USD2.36tn). By March 2016, this increased by 46% to JPY406tn (USD3.44tn).[12]

The scale of the central bank's purchases had never previously been observed. The BOJ assets equated to 70% of the nation's GDP, 45% higher than the US Federal Reserve and ECB assets, which were 25% of their respective GDPs (see Exhibit 1).

The European Experience

Although similar measures were introduced in Denmark, Switzerland, and Sweden between 2012 and 2015, the ECB was the first major European central bank to introduce negative interest rates in June 2014.[13]

Negative interest rates helped to encourage the extension of European bank loans, but it was not certain that similar results would be achieved in Japan, where commercial bank loans were relatively solid. Still, Kuroda believed his policy would lead to increased prices, consumption, and capital expenditure. How negative interest rates would affect Japan was unknown at the time of their introduction, as adverse side effects were known only in the European context. Although European central banks adopted negative interest rates, economists did not agree on the extent to which these succeeded.

Negative interest rates affected a nation's economy in two key areas: they reduced interest rates on loans, which in theory boosted capital and housing investment. They also encouraged a process by which money was transferred from low-yield government bonds to foreign securities. In theory, negative interest rates weakened the Japanese currency and elevated stocks.

---

[11] *Ibid.*

[12] *Ibid.*

[13] "How Does Negative Rate Policy Work," *Japan Times*, 14 August 2019, https://www.japantimes.co.jp/news/2019/08/14/business/negative-rate-policy-work/#.XiPCARMzZjs, accessed 25 February 2020.

Exhibit 1:   Changes in BOJ's Monetary Policy

2010	Policy rate hit "zero lower bound." Lowered short-term nominal interest rate
	Rate
	0%
Mar. 2013	Kuroda assumed office of BOJ Governor
Apr. 2013	BOJ purchased JGBs to lower yield curve. Government bond purchased to lower yield curve % of issued JGB held by BOJ
	40% 30% 20% 10% 0% FY2010 '11 '12 '13 '14 '15
Feb. 2016	Introduction of negative interest rate
	Rate Minus 0.1% rate applied to portion of current-account funds at BOJ
	0%
	–0.1%
Sept. 2016	Introduction of yield-curve control
	Guided 10 year interest rate to around zero
	Rate
	0% Term
	–0.1%
	10-year

Source: S. Tani (29 September 2016). "The Bank of Japan Tries to Bend the Yield Curve," *Nikkei Asian Review*, https://asia.nikkei.com/Economy/The-Bank-of-Japan-tries-to-bend-the-yield-curve, accessed 21 November 2019.

In Europe, their introduction caused a sharp decline in bank lending rates and increased bank lending. However, this was modest at best, since a slowdown in economic activity directly impacted the demand for loans, which decreased by 3% on an annual basis. This trend continued for one year. Additionally, European banks were reluctant to offer high-risk loans, as the low rates they entailed meant they lacked sufficient incentives to enter into risky contracts.

Even where loan growth entered a positive cycle, there was only so much that the demand achieved. Before the slump in crude oil prices, inflation hovered around 0%, and the projected rates remained low in most European countries.

Central bank policies in Europe adversely affected households, especially retirees. In Switzerland, Denmark, and Sweden, people increased their savings in response to rate cuts. They feared low interest rates reduced their retirement savings. There was also an inherent risk that these fears would spread through lack of demand, increased prices, and ultimately, deflation. This was contradictory to the objectives of the central banks involved.

The European experience with negative interest rates was considered to be more serious than Japan's, because Japan's percentage of retirees (age 65 and over) was the highest in the world, at 27.58%, at that time. In Germany, that percentage was 21.46% of citizens, France (20.03%), and the US (15.81%), respectively.[14] Most of those in Japan were recipients of pension funds. Since these incomes were fixed, they tended to save money if the future was uncertain.

Another risk was the effect negative interest rates had on currency markets. A year after the ECB went negative, the euro fell by 18% against the USD in one year,[15] because investors shifted investments from the euro to USD treasury bonds, alternative currencies, and assets.

But a drop in the value of the euro enhanced the profitability of European companies and boosted stock prices by 10%, year-on-year.

---

[14]"Global Aging Rate (Elderly Population Ratio) Changes by Country, 1990–2018," *Global* Note, https://www.globalnote.jp/post-3770.html, accessed 7 May 2020.

[15]The US Dollar/Euro Exchange Rate Was 1.3690 in June 2014 and 1.1188 in June 2015. Bloomberg Currency Converter, https://www.bloomberg.com/markets/currencies, accessed 28 February 2020.

Many economists speculated that the BOJ's real objective was to weaken Japan's currency.[16]

In fact, the BOJ's decision initially caused the JPY to fall and stock prices to rise, but the move was short-lived. Uncertainty about the Chinese and US economies led to a further bout of market turmoil.

Key Differences

Some inherent differences between Japanese and European economies were also of significance.

Although Japan's financial system was stronger than Europe's, Japanese companies and consumers were extremely cautious after two decades of economic decline. Even if interest rates fell further, demand for funds did not increase.

According to Kuroda, the QQE strategy, combined with negative interest rates, represented "the most powerful monetary policy framework in the history of modern central banking."[17] When the central bank adopted this strategy, the BOJ's governor showed he was prepared to take aggressive measures if they were needed.

Kuroda's Strategy

The degree of negative rates introduced by European central banks is bigger than Japan. Technically there definitely is room for a further cut in Japan.

— Haruhiko Kuroda[18]

---

[16]A. Ross, M. Mackenzie, and J. Soble (11 May 2013). "Abenomics Propels Yen Weakness," *Financial Times*, https://www.ft.com/content/dbdc8d5c-b8d9-11e2-869f-00144feabdc0, accessed 28 February 2020.

[17]"Meeting with the Governor," Bank of Japan, 1 February 2016, https://www.boj.or.jp/announcements/press/kaiken_2016/kk1602a.pdf, accessed 20 November 2019.

[18]"Bank of Japan Governor Haruhiko Kuroda Says He Won't Rule Out Deepening Negative Rates: Report," Reuters, 21 August 2016, https://www.cnbc.com/2016/08/21/bank-of-japan-governor-haruhiko-kuroda-says-he-wont-rule-out-deepening-negative-rates-report.html, accessed 29 February 2020.

At first, markets questioned the ability of lenders to manage such a radical strategy.

Aware that some of the central banks in Europe had ventured near to, or even beyond, 0.1%, Kuroda argued that Japan had "sufficient room for further monetary easing in the negative interest rate dimension."[19]

The prospect that interest rates could drop below zero rocked the bond market. Negative yields for newly issued 10-year JGBs were observed for the first time. Investors sold off bank shares. They feared rates that fell below zero had negative ramifications[20]; since banks had a significant role in support of Japan's economy, any concerns about their viability reduced investors' willingness to enter into risky propositions.

The Nikkei 225 Index (Nikkei Stock Average) fell by 24.1% — a move that started the day before the new policy was implemented on 28 January 2016. On average, the Nikkei declined by 7.8% between that date and 11 February 2016.[21]

The negative interest rate affected banks either directly through a bank's BOJ accounts where the impact was relatively minor, as the rate was only narrowly applied due to the tiered nature of the application, or via the yield curve.

The BOJ's policy exerted a strong downward pressure on the entire yield curve, a move that flattened corporate lending margins and reduced financial institutions' revenues. This had a negative impact on lending and the smooth operation of the financial system.

Kuroda's strategy was also viewed positively, since it was obvious that the central bank paid higher prices for the JGBs it purchased from financial institutions, which proved positive for sellers. The money that the BOJ exchanged for JGBs went into the sellers' current accounts, where it had the potential to earn a negative return.

To ensure financial institutions were willing to sell, prices at which the JGBs traded needed to reflect the added cost of a negative interest rate.

---

[19] T. Goto and K. Takami (8 February 2016). "What Europe's Experience Tells Us about the BOJ's Experiment," *Nikkei Asian Review*, https://asia.nikkei.com/Politics-Economy/Economy/What-Europe-s-experience-tells-us-about-the-BOJ-s-experiment, accessed 29 February 2020.

[20] I. Shimizu (11 February 2016). "Markets Weigh Pros, Cons of Joining the Minus 1% Club," *Nikkei Asian Review*, https://asia.nikkei.com/Business/Finance/Markets-weigh-pros-cons-of-joining-the-minus-1-club, accessed 21 November 2019.

[21] *Ibid.*

In addition, the reduction in the long-term interest rates also increased bond purchase prices.

But from a financial institution's perspective, any positive impact that the negative interest rate of 0.1% yielded was outweighed by its negative impact.

Hitting Turbulence

After the BOJ announced its QQE policy, investors exhibited more risk-adverse behavior. In the presence of higher risk, they engaged in safer investments, one of which was the Japanese yen (JPY). In this regard, Abenomics achieved Prime Minister Abe's objective to reduce the value of the JPY, which normally traded at 110 to 115 to the USD, which then traded strongly around JPY110.

Speaking before Congress, US Federal Reserve chair Janet Yellen indicated that US interest rates would not be ramped up in the foreseeable future. But on December 2015, for the first time in nearly a decade, the Fed increased its policy rate, which was near zero. Its decision not to introduce further rate hikes narrowed the gap between the US and Japanese real interest rates, allowing the JPY to gain ground on the USD.

There was an inherent risk that even a slight move into negative territory could have far-reaching consequences. Immediately after the QQE policy was announced, bank stocks fell. Investors were concerned that negative interest rates diminished lenders' earnings. While the policy was designed to reduce lending rates, there was little chance that the deposit rates would also fall because they already bordered on zero. As such, there was a high risk that Kuroda's plan seriously undermined bank profits, which resulted in even less lending.

Controlling the Curve

In order to achieve the price stability target of 2%, it is necessary to drastically convert the deflationary mindset among people and raise inflation expectations.

— Haruhiko Kuroda[22]

---

[22] H. Kuroda (20 June 2016). "Overcoming Deflation: Theory and Practice," Speech given by the Governor of the Bank of Japan, https://www.bis.org/review/r160623a.pdf, accessed 7 May 2020.

Exhibit 2:   Japan's Year-on-Year CPI Growth; All Items, Excluding Fresh Food %

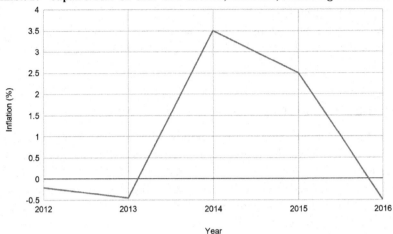

Source: Compiled from Nikkei (29 September 2016). "The Bank of Japan Tries to Bend the Yield Curve," http://asia.nikkei.com/magazine/20160929-ASIA300-MVPs-MAJOR-VALUE-PRODUCERS/Politics-Economy/The-Bank-of-Japan-tries-to-bend-the-yield-curve, accessed 21 November 2019.

For a negative interest rate policy to succeed, Kuroda realized he needed to do more. He decided that the BOJ needed to control the yield curve in order to meet the Abenomics inflation target of 2% and maintain yields on 10-year JGBs, which acted as the foundation of long-term interest rates, at around zero (see Exhibit 2).

In defense of his decision, Kuroda stated, "We have found through our bond purchasing and negative rate policy that the yield curve can be controlled. Deciding the right interest rate level is what central banks have always done. It is not that different."[23]

According to conventional monetary theory, it was not possible to maintain yields in this manner because long-term interest rates were not entirely within the control of a central bank. But the BOJ took financial

---

[23] S. Tani (29 September 2016). "The Bank of Japan Tries to Bend the Yield Curve," *Nikkei Asian Review*, https://asia.nikkei.com/Economy/The-Bank-of-Japan-tries-to-bend-the-yield-curve, accessed 21 November 2019.

engineering to a new level when it introduced yield curve control in an effort to boost Japan's economy.[24]

Other factors, such as fiscal policy, external market conditions, and inflation expectations, all influenced long-term interest rates. Monetary authorities traditionally focused on the factors they controlled, namely short-term interest rates, to stimulate or dampen the economy. It was assumed that to reduce or increase rates at the short end of the yield curve would also impact long-term rates.

While global central banks attempted to reduce long-term interest rates by purchasing government bonds over a longer duration, maintaining their rates at a set level around zero was something entirely different.

Although the bank increased the value of its monetary base by JPY80tn annually, this had predominantly depended on the purchase of JGBs, and these were about to run out. In a statement that tacitly acknowledged these technical limitations, Kuroda revealed that the new framework raised "the sustainability of our monetary easing policy."

Inflation Overshooting Commitment

A new inflation overshooting commitment was designed to maintain inflation at a steady rate. However, no positive result was observed (see Exhibit 3).

An overshooting commitment could, theoretically, lead to actual inflation because the current inflation rate was well below 2%. In August 2016, Japan's year-on-year consumer price index (CPI), which excluded fresh food, declined for the sixth consecutive month.

Although it was too early to look beyond a 2% target, the BOJ's solution was to expand its monetary base, based on the observed CPI inflation rate instead of expected inflation.[25]

---

[24]J. Cox (21 September 2016). "CNBC explains: The Bank of Japan's 'yield curve control,'" *CNBC*, https://www.cnbc.com/2016/09/21/cnbc-explains-the-bank-of-japan-yield-curve-control.html, accessed 28 February 2020.

[25]H. Kuroda (8 October 2016). "Quantitative and Qualitative Monetary Easing (QQE) with Yield Curve Control: New Monetary Policy Framework for Overcoming Low Inflation," Bank of Japan, https://www.boj.or.jp/en/about/press/koen_2016/ko161009a.htm, accessed 3 March 2020.

Exhibit 3:   Monetary Base Relative to Nominal GDP

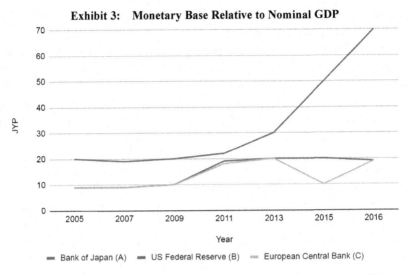

Source: Compiled from Bank of Japan data (https://www.boj.or.jp/) and IMF data (https://www.imf.org/en/Data), accessed 21 November 2019.

The central bank declared it would maintain its easing program as long as needed to achieve and maintain an inflation target of 2% in a stable manner. Although the CPI varied according to cyclical economic fluctuations, movements in the prices of international commodities, and other factors, the central bank said it would not adjust its easing policy, even if the CPI exhibited temporary growth beyond 2%. Inflation needed to reach 2% and remain there for a sustained period before the BOJ considered ending the QQE program. Economists perceived this overshooting commitment to indicate that the BOJ had learned from its previous mistakes.

To achieve 2% inflation, companies needed to give employees wage increases. Employees only perceived a 2% price increase to be natural if their wages also increased by 2% annually.

But to fund higher wages, companies needed to be confident about Japan's future growth. Unfortunately, they lacked confidence, and their low expectations of economic growth stressed the need for structural reform. However, the BOJ alone could not address this issue. This was, perhaps, one of the most significant lessons of the QQE with the negative interest rate policy.

The Limits of Central Banking

Problems with monetary policy were not confined to Japan. In August 2016, US Federal Reserve chair Janet Yellen mentioned that fiscal policies and structural reforms could play an important role in enhancing the strength of the economy.[26] Her European counterpart, Mario Draghi, president of the ECB, had previously stressed that monetary policy alone was not sufficient to achieve balanced growth.[27]

Kuroda agreed.[28] He said, "The BOJ believes that its monetary policy and the government's fiscal policy, as well as initiatives for strengthening Japan's growth potential, would navigate Japan's economy toward overcoming deflation and achieving sustainable growth."[29] The question remained as to whether its policy framework would help the BOJ achieve its 2% inflation target, and whether this was a viable monetary policy tool for central banks.

His strategy was inherently risky, and the credibility of the BOJ stood to be damaged if it was forced to depend on increasingly complicated monetary policies to ensure its actions benefited Japan's economy.

By September 2016, the US Fed and the BOJ had adopted very different positions. The BOJ struggled to ease monetary policy, while the Fed struggled to reduce monetary accommodation. Although their strategies

---

[26] J.L. Yellen (26 August 2016). "The Federal Reserve's Monetary Policy Toolkit: Past, Present, and Future," Federal Reserve, https://www.federalreserve.gov/newsevents/speech/yellen20160826a.htm, accessed 1 March 2020.

[27] M. Draghi (14 December 2015). "Monetary Policy and Structural Reforms in the Euro Area," European Central Bank, https://www.ecb.europa.eu/press/key/date/2015/html/sp151214.en.html, accessed 1 March 2020.

[28] H. Kuroda, "Quantitative and Qualitative Monetary Easing (QQE) with Yield Curve Control": New Monetary Policy Framework for Overcoming Low Inflation," Bank of Japan, Speech at the Brookings Institution in Washington, D.C., 8 October 2016, https://www.brookings.edu/wp-content/uploads/2016/09/1610-governor-kuroda_brookings.pdf, accessed 20 November 2019.

[29] M. Misawa (2016). "Sales Tax Increase in 2014 Under Abenomics: The Japanese Government's Dilemma," The University of Hong Kong, Ref. 15/563C, http://www.acrc.org.hk/, accessed 20 November 2019.

differed, both central banks agreed that monetary policy alone could not be used to address complicated economic scenarios.

The US Fed's decision to leave interest rates on hold was simpler than the BOJ's interventionist policy. The Fed waited for evidence that the labor market and the US economy were sufficiently robust before it influenced interest rates. It wanted to be sure that the US economy weathered uncertainties elsewhere, particularly in Europe and China. On face value, the Fed saw positive signs. Participation rates rose and consumer spending increased slowly. However, warning signs, in the form of capital investment trends and a major inventory correction, significantly reduced domestic growth. If the inventory problem was resolved, there was a chance capital spending could be revived. If US President Donald Trump's administration embraced higher investment spending, higher interest rates would occur.

In December 2016, the world's central banks doubted that they had the tools to boost the real economy and deliver inflation targets. Unlike the US, the BOJ didn't have to contend with the politics that surrounded the US Fed. But its job was no easier. In September 2016, the BOJ announced two new policies. It wanted inflation not just to meet its 2% target, but to overshoot it. To do this it targeted short-term interest rates and long-term government bond yields.[30]

Would Abenomics Reinvigorate Japan's Economy?

The BOJ aimed to expand its monetary base until inflation exceeded the 2% target and remained at that level for a prolonged period. It announced that it would achieve a 0% yield on 10-year JGBs while it invested JPY80tn (USD678bn) in bonds, every year. This move was designed to demonstrate that the central bank intended to hit its inflation target. Such a commitment looked somewhat optimistic given that the monetary base had increased by 300% since Abenomics emerged in December 2012.

There was also a lack of clarity about the BOJ's actual target. The central bank effectively adopted a price target for 10-year JGBs at zero yield, because bond price and yield were inversely related.

---

[30]G. Ip (21 September 2016). "Central Bank Tools Are Losing Their Edge," *Wall Street Journal*, https://www.wsj.com/articles/central-bank-tools-are-losing-their-edge-1474501934, accessed 1 March 2020.

Although the bank set a quantity target, to purchase JPY80tn of bonds a year, the price or yield still varied. Therefore, one of its targets needed to be relinquished because it was not possible to simultaneously focus on price and quantity.

In reality, the BOJ had six targets:

- A price target for JGBs
- A quantity target for JGBs
- Negative interest rates at –0.1%
- Use of the JPY as a transmission mechanism to inflation
- 2% or more inflation
- A steeper yield curve (or higher interest rates for longer-dated bonds)

The steeper yield curve was derived from efforts to maintain 10-year yields at zero while longer-dated JGB yields increased. This enhanced the profitability of the banks and helped insurance firms that were struggling in the negative rate environment because both invested in JGBs. If longer-dated JGB yields increased, their returns on the investments improved.

Unless the central bank or Japan's government engineered a sustained GDP increase and higher inflation, investors continued to buy longer-term bonds and, contrary to the BOJ's objectives, this flattened the yield curve.

The US Fed and the BOJ did, however, have something in common. Both failed to stimulate the type of inflation that was required to back away from overtly easy monetary accommodation. All central banks shared the same issue.

To some extent, monetary accommodation made issues much worse for central banks. People had no choice but to save when they were concerned that the value of their money had diminished. Those who did not have significant pensions were motivated to save more to cover their retirement. Operating in isolation, central banks were not able to deliver the solid economic changes needed to turn the situation around.

Abenomics was not groundbreaking. Since Japan's real estate bubble burst in the late 1980s, the government had implemented programs designed to secure near-zero interest rates. It invested billions of yen in its efforts to improve the economy and had subsequently accumulated one of the world's highest public debts.

Shinzo Abe believed Abenomics would break this cycle, reduce exchange rates, and give the export trade market a much-needed boost. As he had anticipated, the JPY did initially fall against the USD, by as much as 50% at one point. But this failed to increase exports, and the stock market remained volatile.

A weaker JPY was not necessarily positive, as it drove up import prices and reduced consumer demand and spending. Global oil prices reached record lows, down from more than USD100 a barrel to USD30 a barrel between 2014 and 2016. This only added to Japan's deflation problem. Eventually, a combination of cheap oil and a stagnant world economy reduced any chance that Japan's economy could recover from its deflationary spiral.

Critics of Abenomics pointed out that the policy enhanced risk, without any benefit. They believed monetary easing spurred hyperinflation or did little to reverse a systematic deflationary mindset. Japan's national debt, which reached more than USD11tn, represented more than 245% of the country's GDP (see Exhibit 3).

The International Monetary Fund (IMF) warned Japan that its debt levels could not be sustained and that structural reforms were needed: "Without additional reforms, Japan risks falling back into lower growth and deflation, a further deterioration in the fiscal situation, and an overreliance on monetary stimulus with negative consequences for the region."[31] To reduce the deficit, Prime Minister Abe increased Japan's taxes, a move that undermined the objectives of the program.[32]

The national consumption tax that increased from 5% to 8% in 2014 further reduced consumer spending and was blamed for a renewed recession.[33] A planned increase to 10% was postponed as a result of the 2014 performance.[34] Although this decision aimed to encourage growth, it potentially went against the fiscal sustainability goal.

Negative interest rates unsettled global economists. Kuroda accepted that there was every chance his policy could damage the banking system

---

[31]"Asia and Pacific: Sustaining the Momentum: Vigilance and Reforms," *IMF Regional Economic Outlook*, April 2014, https://www.imf.org/en/Publications/REO/APAC/Issues/2017/02/23/Sustaining-the-Momentum-Vigilance-and-Reforms, accessed 20 November 2019.

[32]Supra note 23.

[33]*Ibid.*

[34]*Ibid.*

and cause Japan's citizens to hoard cash at home, which added to deflation.

Decision Time

Nine months after Kuroda made his announcement that the BOJ would adopt QQE with negative interest rates in January 2016, the BOJ reviewed its plan and changed direction, from a focus on the quantity of the monetary base to a renewed emphasis on interest rates.

Just when the BOJ would achieve a 2% inflation target remained a key question. Its purchases of JGBs had reached double the volume of the new debt issued by the government. However, this was not enough to stop a rapid reduction in consumer prices. In 2016, prices fell at the fastest rate since the introduction of QE in 2013.

The BOJ's unconventional policies and tools appeared to have failed. When the central bank hit the zero lower bound — in theory, the lower limit of interest rates is zero — it found itself with no room to reduce nominal short-term interest rates, so it engaged in aggressive government bond purchases, a move that reduced rates across all periods.

As purchases neared their limit, the bank implemented a negative interest rate policy. This strategy was considered by the market to be unthinkable, because it undercut the bank's asset purchasing program. But this time, the BOJ leveraged a head-on challenge to monetary theory. In light of the bank's unsuccessful track record, markets were uneasy and speculation was rife that even more unconventional measures would emerge (see Exhibit 3).

Kuroda now had to deal with a number of serious dilemmas.

1. *BOJ Control of Long-Term Rates*

Although the 2% inflationary target had been set more than three years earlier, it had not been achieved, and at the same time, the amount of Japanese bonds the BOJ purchased neared its limit. The bank realized it needed to aim for its inflation target over a longer period of time. Setting this at 0% could be achieved without the bank buying as many government bonds.

The long stagnation of the real economy caused a shift in the portfolios of commercial banks from lenders to JGBs. The portfolio shift was caused by a fall in the ratio of the loan rate to unit lending costs, or the bank's price-cost margin for lending.[35]

Abenomics required that banks lend more money to industries and consumers increase investment and consumption to stimulate growth. The government did not welcome the banks' shift from loans to JGBs. As long as the BOJ bought JGBs, banks bought and held more JGBs. This created a dilemma for the BOJ. Could the BOJ continue along this path?

2. The BOJ Recognized That Quantitative Expansion Was Limited but Was Still a Viable Method to Ease Interest Rates. Could This Approach Be Successful?

Although there seemed reasonable scope to implement negative rates in Europe, this was not the case in Japan. It was feasible to cut rates to −1%, but because the profit margins of Japanese financial institutions were smaller than their European counterparts, adverse effects on bank earnings were more pronounced. The matter could not be resolved via the same strategy used in Europe.

3. The BOJ Adopted a Forward Guidance Policy to Expand the Monetary Base until It Reached Its 2% Target. Could This Be Sustained?

To raise inflationary expectations, the bank adopted a forward guidance policy, and adjusted the 2% inflation target to an inflationary goal of over 2%. Without an increase in the money supply, the policy lacked credibility and was not sustainable over the long term. Even if the policy were successful, problems managing long-term interest rates might have emerged when inflation breached 2%; as such, the policy was also not sustainable.

---

[35]K. Ogawa and K. Imai (2014). "Why Do Commercial Banks Hold Government Bonds? The Case of Japan," *Journal of the Japanese and International Economies* 34, 201–216, https://www.sciencedirect.com/science/article/pii/S0889158314000471, accessed 1 March 2020.

4. If the BOJ Improved the Sustainability of Its Monetary Policy, Could It Continue to Contribute to Economic Policy?

If the BOJ implemented a policy that successfully addressed deflation and economic stagnation, it would continue to play an important role in economic policy. However, because of the protracted nature of the problem and the policy's failure to bring about inflation, options narrowed for the central bank. This limited its future role.

5. What if Further Interest Rate Reductions Failed to Stimulate the Economy?

The belief that lowering rates beyond zero into negative territory would stimulate the economy was inaccurate. The impact on bank earnings impaired the ability of financial institutions to lend to the real economy, and damaged the money-creation aspect of fractional banking, a key element of credit creation in developed economies. There was also a negative impact on insurance and pension asset management. Falling interest rates also made workers risk-averse.

6. With Limited Options for Easing, Should the BOJ Work with Government?

With little room for easing, the BOJ needed to work with the government's fiscal policy. Options included the use of so-called helicopter money or, at the very least, the application of a supportive monetary policy in conjunction with government fiscal policy. The central bank could also use its influence to press for supply-side reform, the missing element in Prime Minister Abe's economic policy.

7. How Did Helicopter Money Work?

Helicopter money, in the form of long-term bonds issued by the government, was accompanied by a commitment from the BOJ to hold bonds for a protracted period. The government could even issue perpetual bonds, i.e., completely nonredeemable bonds, directly to the central bank. This meant the government printed money. However, such a move risked hyperinflation and a volatile devaluation of the currency in the future.

The BOJ's QQE could target other asset purchases, such as municipal bonds, or the debt of state-backed companies where intervention would have more impact, or the deep and liquid treasury bond market (which bought JPY80tn of JGBs each year). Compared to this market, the municipal bond market was characterized by low volume and illiquidity, giving the BOJ a greater chance to distort it. Pumped prime, these markets introduced an upward price bias, and as the bank continued its purchases at inflated rates, this was a close approximation of helicopter money.

The final option was a special BOJ account that the government would always have the ability to borrow from by committing to purchase a large portion of government debt or buying corporate bonds. This also represented a form of helicopter money.

Owing to the risk of future high inflation as a result of creating a money supply that allowed the government to implement its fiscal policy, the BOJ refrained from supporting a helicopter money policy.

8. What if the BOJ Purchased Perpetual or Foreign Bonds?

Issuing zero-coupon bonds or replacing bonds held by the bank with non-redeemable perpetual bonds offered a cost-free form of financing for the government and, if the bonds were parked on the central bank's balance sheet, increased its ability to stimulate the economy with fiscal policy.

The large-scale purchase of foreign bonds was another alternative, which would exert a downward pressure on the JPY, an outcome Prime Minister Abe desired because it would stimulate Japanese exports.

Both policies faced legal hurdles. Perpetual bonds fell foul of Article 5 of the Public Finance Law of Japan, which forbid the central bank from underwriting public debt. In addition, the Bank of Japan Act outlawed the purchase of foreign bonds as a means of currency intervention. But there was some room to maneuver with perpetual bonds. If the amount was limited by the Diet and only used for the purchase of foreign bonds, it could be carried out under the guise of monetary policy.

In 2016, faced with intractable deflation and perpetual economic stagnation, Haruhiko Kuroda admitted that monetary policy had reached the limits of its effectiveness.

This led to greater cooperation with the government in order to lend greater traction to reflation policies. Kuroda thought small tweaks to the framework would satisfy the market's desire for action, but there was no easy solution. He felt that it was better to recognize the limitations of monetary policy when attempting to stimulate an economy entrenched in a deep malaise, rather than attempt ever more unconventional forms of monetary stimulus.

The conclusion Kuroda reached was that it was reasonable to expect the BOJ to maintain inflation close to target in normal economic circumstances, but given the depth of Japan's problem, monetary policy alone could not be expected to solve a deep-seated problem.

Fears of Recession

Kuroda's term was due to end in April 2018, and although it looked as though he would leave office before he achieved his primary goal, in a vote of confidence, he was reappointed by Japan's government for a second five-year term.

Despite the BOJ's efforts to work with government, the nation had moved toward recession by early 2020. When the consumption tax was eventually raised to 10% in 2019, it sparked the biggest quarterly contraction since 2014,[36] as households reacted against the dual effects of minor wage gains and budgetary pressures. Although the move was unpopular, it fulfilled the government's dual needs: to pay for pensions and healthcare for Japan's rapidly aging population, and to rein in the developed world's largest debt.[37]

For Further Discussion

(1) What is a deflationary spiral and what caused this issue in Japan?
(2) Define deflation, disinflation, inflation, reflation, and stagflation.
(3) How does the BOJ's quantitative and qualitative monetary easing policy relate to the expected inflation theory?

---

[36]"Japan Suffers Worst Economic Slump in Five Years," *Agence France-Press*, 17 February 2020, https://www.afp.com/en/news/15/japan-suffers-worst-economic-slump-five-years-doc-1p21on1, accessed 17 February 2020.

[37]Y. Takeo and S. Ito (25 February 2020). "History Repeats as Sales Tax Hike Pushes Japan towards Recession," *Bloomberg*, https://www.bloomberg.com/news/articles/2020-02-24/history-repeats-as-sales-tax-hike-pushes-japan-toward-recession?srnd=premium-asia, accessed 25 February 2020.

(4) Explain the implications of negative interest rates on Japan and the underpinnings of the BOJ's decision to implement them?

(5) How does helicopter monetary policy differ from traditional quantitative easing?

(6) The BOJ was arguably the most likely central bank to adopt a helicopter money policy. Was this policy feasible in the Japanese context?

(7) The former US Federal Reserve Chairman Ben Bernanke suggests the use of perpetual bonds to the Abe administration. How do these work?

Case 6

Rethinking Saizeriya's Currency Hedging Strategy[*]

The success of popular Italian fast-food chain Saizeriya with Japanese consumers led to the company's public listing in Tokyo and a significant expansion into new markets in Asia, where its affordable restaurant menus included pizzas, pasta, and seafood, as well as rice dishes. Many of the ingredients included in its meals were sourced from Australian suppliers. The company had grown to around 1,500 businesses, which operated as subsidiaries, branches, and franchises, and the company planned for further growth.

The company's long-standing president, Issei Horino, was appointed to the position of representative director on Saizeriya's board in 2000. The silver-haired, 63-year-old corporate veteran became the multinational company's president in 2009, taking over the role from its founder, Yasuhiko Shogaki, who established the company in 1973. Although he relinquished his position as company president in 2009, Shogaki continued to be involved in Saizeriya's operations, as chairman of its board.

Faced with economic uncertainty that looked likely to continue, Issei Horino felt he needed to strengthen and create greater stability for the

[*] Professor Mitsuru Misawa from the University of Hawaii at Manoa prepared this case for class discussion. This case is not intended to show effective or ineffective handling of decision or business processes. The author might have disguised certain information to protect confidentiality. Cases are written in the past tense, this is not meant to imply that all practices, organizations, people, places, or facts mentioned in the case no longer occur, exist, or apply.

company as its share price in Japan, together with its profitability, had fallen.[1] He was particularly concerned about costs associated with payments to the firm's Australian suppliers, since these were paid in Australian dollars (AUD).

Horino wondered if Saizeriya could use currency hedging to avoid financial losses and manage costs caused by unexpected fluctuations in exchange rates. He knew that Shogaki had previously used this method, and that the former president's decision resulted in near financial disaster for the company, in addition to costly court cases. Horino wondered if, by careful examination of all the steps the company took with its previous foreign currency coupon swaps, he could avoid the same mistakes and effectively use currency hedging as a tool to better manage the company's risks associated with the depreciation of the Japanese yen (JPY).

Fast and Affordable

As a catering business headquartered in Yoshikawa, Saizeriya sold Italian-style meals at affordable prices to its customers (see Exhibits 1 and 2).[2,3] It maintained a high-quality menu with low prices through a uniform production and sales system that covered everything from the procurement of ingredients to service at its 1,517 restaurants throughout Japan and overseas. The company opened its first outlet in China in 2003, and by the end of the Japanese financial year (1 September 2019–31 August 2020), nearly a third of the restaurants it operated were located in Singapore, Hong Kong SAR, Shanghai, Guangzhou, Beijing, and China Taiwan.[4]

The company also expanded into fast-food restaurants. Its hamburger chain, Eat Run, opened in 2005, and the pasta outlet, Saizeriya Express,

---

[1] S. Tanabe, "Japan's Saizeriya Takes Slice of China's Food Scene with $3 Pizza," *Nikkei Asia*, https://asia.nikkei.com/Business/Food-Beverage/Japan-s-Saizeriya-takes-slice-of-China-s-food-scene-with-3-pizza, accessed 28 December 2020.

[2] Saizeriya (26 November 2020). "To Our Shareholders and Investors," https://www.saizeriya.co.jp/corporate/en/investor/ir/, accessed 1 December 2020.

[3] Y. Shogaki (2016). "Saizeriya Doesn't Sell because It's Delicious. It's Delicious Food That Sells!," *Nikkei Business*, pp. 1–10.

[4] Saizeriya, "Annual Report 2020," https://www.saizeriya.co.jp/PDF/irpdf000939.pdf, accessed 29 January 2021.

Exhibit 1:   Saizeriya's Corporate Data (as of 31 August 2020)

Corporate Name:	Saizeriya Co. Ltd.
Head Office:	2-5 Asahi, Yoshikawa-city, Saitama 342-0008, Japan
Established:	1 May 1973
Common Stock:	JPY8,612bn
Number of Shares Issued:	52,272,342 shares
Fiscal Year-End:	31 August 2020
Securities Code Number:	7581 (T.S.E., 1st Sec.)
Business Lines:	Italian-style restaurant chain
Number of Employees:	4,164
Chairman:	Yasuhiko Shogaki
President:	Issei Horino

Source: Saizeriya, "Saizeriya Data File 2020," https://www.saizeriya.co.jp/corporate/information/outline/, accessed 28 November 2020.

opened its doors in 2007.[5] The firm's 2020 annual report stated that it employed 4,164 full-time employees across all of its markets, on a consolidated basis[6] (those it employed at its headquarters, branches, and wholly owned subsidiaries).

Since 2003, meals and ingredients were manufactured at Saizeriya's operations in Melton, Australia,[7] where its factory sourced high-quality local raw ingredients, which it processed into ready-made sauces, soups, and meat, free of artificial colors or flavors.

Managing Profitability in Downturns

Our principal initiatives are to develop attractive products unique to Saizeriya and enhance quality and productivity through technological improvement. At the same time, we will emphasize initiatives that lead to corporate sustainability, such as measures against waste loss and

---

[5] Saizeriya, "About Us," https://www.saizeriya.com.sg/company/, accessed 28 December 2020.

[6] *Ibid.*

[7] Saizeriya, "Welcome to Saizeriya Australia," http://www.saizeriya.com.au/index.html, accessed 28 December 2020.

Exhibit 2: Saizeriya's Financial Results for the Year Ended 31 August 2020 (Consolidated)

Income Statement	FY to 31 Aug. 2020 Amount (JPY) Million	Net Sales Ratio	FY to 31 Aug. 2019 Amount (JPY) Million	Net Sales Ratio	Difference
Net Sales	126,842	100%	156,527	100%	—
Sales Cost	47,397	37.4%	56,277	36%	1.4%
Gross Margin	79,445	62.6%	100,250	64%	-1.4%
Selling, General, and Administrative Expenses	83,260	65.6%	90,651	57.9%	7.7%
Operating Income	-3,815	—	9,599	6.1%	—
Ordinary Income	-2,091	—	9,731	6.2%	—
Net Income for This Year	-3,450	—	4,980	3.2%	—

Source: Saizeriya (October 14, 2020). "Financial Results Briefing Session for the Fiscal Year Ended 31 August 2020," Code No. 7581, https://www.saizeriya.co.jp/PDF/irpdf000882.pdf, accessed 28 November 2020.

energy savings and environmental measures at our outlets, plants, and farms.

— Issei Horino, President, Saizeriya[8]

With ongoing economic uncertainty likely to continue to impact the company's profitability, Horino decided to examine the company's material procurement[9] strategy to discover if he could reduce its costs through currency hedging.

Yasuhiko Shogaki used foreign currency coupon swaps in October 2007 and February 2008, but that decision resulted in considerable losses to the company. Although Saizeriya blamed the French international banking group BNP Paribas (BNP) for this loss, Horino wondered if his company's management had been at fault. He decided to review Shogaki's use of a derivative known as a foreign currency coupon swap. Horino knew the firm used hedging to reduce costs associated with its essential Australian operations, but the result had risked the company's future.

Although the Australian factory provided high-quality ingredients, it also caused Saizeriya to hold AUD-denominated accounts payable. These were paid in AUD at a future date. Saizeriya needed to protect its vital source of supply from the large currency fluctuations that frequently occurred between the JPY and the AUD. Horino realized that the derivative that Shogaki had entered into also had the potential to create a profit for the company, under certain conditions.

If it used currency hedging, the company did well only if the JPY depreciated against the AUD, and Horino noted that the JPY had fallen since March 2020, when the global coronavirus pandemic (COVID-19) started to have a global impact (see Exhibit 3).

Japan experienced its first COVID-19 cases in January 2020, and the economic impact started to be felt in March 2020. In the fiscal year to 31 August 2020, Saizeriya announced annual sales of JPY126.842bn, an

---

[8] Supra note 4.

[9] Saizeriya, "Effort for Reasonable Price," https://www.saizeriya.co.jp/corporate/effort/, accessed 5 December 2020.

Exhibit 3:   AUD to JPY Exchange Rate, 2020

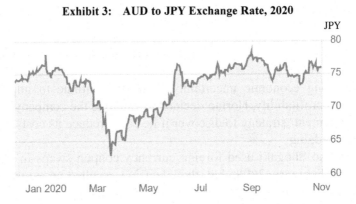

Source: Yahoo! Finance, "Currency Converter," https://finance.yahoo.com/currency-converter/, accessed 25 November 2020.

18.96% drop in just one year. Net income was negative JPY3.45bn, a fall of 169.27% year-on-year (see Exhibit 2).[10]

As the pandemic negatively affected the company's income, Horino was concerned about future losses if the JPY continued to depreciate. Given that scenario, Horino thought that foreign currency hedging was needed to reduce risks and cut costs. But he knew that technique had previously failed,[11] so he wanted to avoid mistakes,[12] particularly since the pandemic had already decimated corporate sales and people's incomes.

In order to protect its reputation and the community, Saizeriya's management wanted to protect the well-being of its customers during the pandemic. In July 2020, it announced that it would raise its prices for 140 different menu items by just one yen.[13] This move resulted in fewer coins and change being handled — an important health precaution; and Horino himself personally demonstrated how customers could use the traditional Japanese paper-folding technique of origami to convert paper napkins

---

[10] Saizeriya (26 November 2020). "To Our Shareholders and Investors," https://www.saizeriya.co.jp/corporate/en/investor/ir/, accessed 1 December 2020.

[11] *Ibid.*

[12] Saizeriya, "2019 Annual Report," https://www.saizeriya.co.jp/PDF/irpdf000895.pdf, accessed 5 December 2020.

[13] C. Baseel (24 July 2020). "Coronavirus Makes Popular Japanese Restaurant Chain Raise Prices by One Yen, but Not to Earn More," *Japan Today*, https://japantoday.com/category/features/food/coronavirus-makes-popular-japanese-restaurant-chain-raise-prices-by-one-yen-but-not-to-earn-more, accessed 5 December 2020.

provided within its restaurants into face masks. This allowed wearers to eat meals while they wore a mask. The company hoped its caring approach would help to prevent the airborne spread of the virus and would reassure those who ate at Saizeriya's outlets that the highest standards of hygiene were met.

Delving into the Past

In October 2020, Horino examined the company's October 2007 and February 2008 hedging contracts with BNP,[14,15] when the company had previously attempted to reduce variability in its cash-flow obligations in response to exchange rate fluctuations. Like many other large Japanese firms, Saizeriya used hedging as a tool to manage its currency exposures.

Horino noted that the currency hedging decision was based on the assumption that Saizeriya's management team would be more severely criticized by shareholders for foreign exchange losses than they would have been if the company incurred financial costs via the implementation of a hedging strategy. He noted that foreign exchange losses were visible on the firm's income statement, but costs associated with hedging were buried within the group's operating expenses.

Normally, the company followed a currency-switching strategy by which it paid foreign debt with JPY, its home currency. But since Australian suppliers often refused to accept JPY as payment, management opted for an alternative payment method — foreign currency coupon swaps to reduce costs associated with currency fluctuations. For example, in 2009, Australian payments accounted for JPY3.987bn, or 13.18% of the company's total manufacturing costs.[16]

Horino understood that Shogaki entered into two foreign currency coupon swap contracts with BNP in an attempt to reduce costs that

[14] Saizeriya, "Effort for Reasonable Price," https://www.saizeriya.co.jp/corporate/effort/, accessed 5 December 2020.

[15] Saizeriya, "2020 Annual Report," https://www.saizeriya.co.jp/PDF/irpdf000895.pdf, accessed 5 December 2020.

[16] Saizeriya (1 December 2009). "Data File 2009," https://www.saizeriya.co.jp/corporate/en/investor/ir/index.php?pageNum=4, accessed 28 November 2020.

Exhibit 4:   AUD to JPY Exchange Rate, 2007–2010

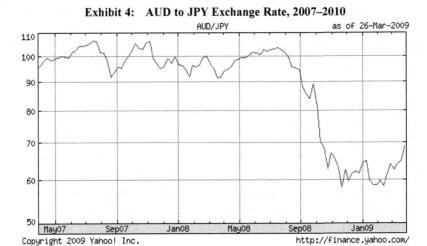

Source: Yahoo! Finance, "Currency Converter," http://finance.yahoo.com/currency-converter/# from=USD to=EUR;amt=1, accessed 5 December 2020.

stemmed from exchange rate fluctuations between the JPY and the AUD[17] (see Exhibit 4). He also observed that the company relied on BNP as its source of advice on how to reduce variability in cash-flow obligations that resulted from variations in exchange rates.

Next, he discovered that Shogaki had entered into contracts for a new derivative known as a foreign currency coupon swap, a tool that was also used by other Japanese companies at that time. Common hedging methods[18] included:

- Forward hedging
- Money-market hedging
- Option hedging

---

[17] Saizeriya (10 December 2008). "Notice Concerning Termination of Derivative Contracts," https://www.saizeriya.co.jp/PDF/irpdf000108.pdf, accessed 20 December 2020.

[18] M. Misawa (2014). "Saizeriya and the Use of Foreign Currency Coupon Swaps: Was This for Hedging or Speculation?" Asian Case Research Centre, The University of Hong Kong, Ref. 14/538C; Saizeriya, 2020 Annual Report, https://www.saizeriya.co.jp/PDF/irpdf000895.pdf, accessed 5 December 2020.

By entering into this derivative, Shogaki had speculated on the potential for the JPY to depreciate in the future. If that had occurred, the company would have benefited from hedging because it would have been able to buy AUD much more cheaply than by other common hedging methods. But what actually happened was that the JPY appreciated.

Horino understood that forecasting exchange rates created uncertainty, and that betting in one direction was speculation. Although the company intended to benefit from hedging, the resultant loss was due to speculation as the JPY appreciated against the AUD over the two-year period of the arrangement (see Exhibit 4). Horino noticed that if Shogaki had not approved the currency swap arrangement, Saizeriya would have enjoyed the benefits of the JPY's appreciation against its AUD-denominated payments. In 2009, a year after these losses, Shogaki stood down as the company's president, and Issei Horino stepped into the role.

Saizeriya's contracts with BNP Paribas meant the company received AUD1mn every month, JPY payments that started in September 2008 (see Exhibit 5). If the JPY weakened below the level set in the contract at JPY78/AUD, the company was entitled to buy AUD at a discount. But if the JPY appreciated beyond the threshold of JPY78/AUD as stated in the contract, the purchase price rose and the company had to buy AUD at a premium (see Exhibits 5 and 6). At that time, the AUD hovered around JPY62.[19]

Horino noted that the total loss that the company incurred due to this particular transaction was JPY8.727bn at JPY65/AUD, over two years. Given that the AUD had weakened to below JPY60 for two years, the company's swap loss was likely to grow to around JPY10.031bn, based on the AUD/JPY60 (see Exhibits 7 and 8) had Shogaki decided not to break the company's contracts with BNP. By breaking the contracts, Shogaki estimated the company's losses would cost JPY15bn. But in its subsequent court cases, he sought restitution of JPY16.8bn, a figure he believed was needed to cover expensive litigation.

Losses and Litigation

While he reviewed the company's documents, Horino noted another crucial management decision. On 9 December 2008, Shogaki announced that

---

[19]At the rate of AUD62/JPY on 9 December 2008.

Exhibit 5:   Contracts of Derivative Transactions between Saizeriya and BNP Paribas

Saizeriya informed the public that it anticipated the valuation loss on derivative transactions for the first quarter of the fiscal year that ended in August 2009 (1 September 2008 to 31 August 2009).[a]

Reason for Potential Valuation Loss on Derivative Transactions
The company ascertained that huge valuation losses on derivative transactions were anticipated for the fiscal year ending August 2009 as non-operating expenses on a non-consolidated basis. The reason was a sharp appreciation of the JPY was anticipated at the end of November 2008, in comparison to the level at fiscal year ended 31 August 2008, which was caused by the volatile fluctuation in the exchange rate resulting from the unprecedented financial crisis.

Amount of Potential Valuation Loss on Derivative Transactions
The amount of potential valuation loss was approximately JPY13bn (AUD0.21bn at the rate of JPY62/AUD on 9 December 2008).

Principal Terms and Conditions of the Derivative Agreements
The counterparty was BNP Paribas Securities (Japan) Ltd.

FX (Foreign Exchange) Reference Type AUD Currency Coupon Swap
The amount of potential valuation loss was JPY8.73bn (AUD0.14bn at the rate of JPY62/AUD on 9 December 2008), based on the estimated rate of JPY65/AUD

1. Agreed date: 22 October 2007.
2. Middle rate as of the last date of agreed month (the end of October 2007) = JPY105.83/AUD.
3. Payment dates: On the first day of each month during the term from 1 December 2008 to 1 November 2010.
4. Agreed amount: AUD1mn.
5. Agreed rate: First agreed rate: JPY78/AUD.

If the JPY became stronger below JPY78/AUD in the FX rate, the agreed rate thereafter would be recalculated in the following manner:

[Previous agreed rate] × [JPY78/FX] = The agreed rate (JPY/AUD)
Minimum = JPY78/AUD, Maximum = JPY600/AUD

1. FX above = Middle rate of JPY/AUD exchange rate at 3 p.m. (Tokyo time) on each foreign exchange reference date.
2. Foreign exchange reference date above was the business day that was five business days before each payment date.

Note: [a]Saizeriya (10 December 2008). "Notice Concerning Termination of Derivative Contracts," https://www.saizeriya.co.jp/PDF/irpdf000108.pdf, accessed 20 December 2020.

Exhibit 6:   Monthly Transaction of Forex Derivatives (Swaps) for the Month of December 2008 at JPY65/AUD

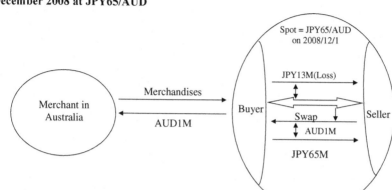

Note: M = million.

exchange rate volatility was likely to result in major instability in the future. To prevent this occurrence, Saizeriya's founder declared that he had decided to dissolve the contracts, although termination would cost the company JPY15bn,[20] payment of which was financed with the company's own money and bank loans.[21]

Although the company's net income in 2008 was JPY4.011bn,[22] the loss that resulted from the termination of contracts could have wiped out the firm's annual income. In 2008, its net assets were JPY54.3542bn,[23] and faced with substantial loss attributed to this particular decision, the company either had to sell off business units or face bankruptcy. Even though it cost the Saizeriya JPY15bn, Shogaki believed his decision to terminate the contracts with BNP saved the company[24] he'd created in 1973.

---

[20] AUD0.24bn at the rate of AUD62/JPY on 9 December 2008.

[21] Saizeriya (22 July 2015). "Deribatibu deno Sonsitsu" ["Loss due to Derivatives"], *Kyodo News*, https://web.archive.org/web/20150722175247/http://www.47news.jp/CN/200811/CN2008112101000884.html, accessed 5 December 2020.

[22] Saizeriya (1 December 2009). "Data File 2009," https://www.saizeriya.co.jp/corporate/en/investor/ir/index.php?pageNum=4, accessed 28 November 2020.

[23] *Ibid.*

[24] Saizeriya (10 December 2009). "Notice on Potential Valuation Loss from Derivative Transactions," https://www.saizeriya.co.jp/PDF/irpdf000113.pdf, accessed 28 November 2020.

Exhibit 7:   Analysis of Swap at JPY65/AUD

Date	Amount	Spot (JPY/AUD)	Effective Rate due to the Contract (JPY/AUD)	Profit/Loss (JPY)
1 Dec 2008	1,000,000	65	78	−13,000,000[a]
1 Jan 2009	1,000,000	65	93.6[b]	−28,600,000
1 Feb 2009	1,000,000	65	112.3[c]	−47,300,000
1 Mar 2009	1,000,000	65	134.8[d]	−69,800,000
1 Apr 2009	1,000,000	65	161.7[e]	−96,700,000
1 May 2009	1,000,000	65	194.0[f]	−129,000,000
1 Jun 2009	1,000,000	65	232.9[g]	−167,900,000
1 Jul 2009	1,000,000	65	279.5[h]	−214,500,000
1 Aug 2009	1,000,000	65	335.4[i]	−270,400,000
1 Sep 2009	1,000,000	65	402.5[j]	−337,500,000
1 Oct 2009	1,000,000	65	483.0[k]	−418,000,000
1 Nov 2009	1,000,000	65	579.6[l]	−514,600,000
1 Dec 2009	1,000,000	65	600[m]	−535,000,000
1 Jan 2010	1,000,000	65	600	−535,000,000
1 Feb 2010	1,000,000	65	600	−535,000,000
1 Mar 2010	1,000,000	65	600	−535,000,000
1 Apr 2010	1,000,000	65	600	−535,000,000
1 May 2010	1,000,000	65	600	−535,000,000
1 Jun 2010	1,000,000	65	600	−535,000,000
1 Jul 2010	1,000,000	65	600	−535,000,000
1 Aug 2010	1,000,000	65	600	−535,000,000
1 Sep 2010	1,000,000	65	600	−535,000,000
1 Oct 2010	1,000,000	65	600	−535,000,000
1 Nov 2010	1,000,000	65	600	−535,000,000
Total				−8,727,300,000

Notes: [a](65 × 1,000,000) − (78 × 1,000,000) = −13,000,000; [b]78 × 78/65 = 78 × 1.2 = 93.6; [c]93.6 × 78/65 = 93.6 × 1.2 = 112.3; [d]112.3 × 1.2 = 134.8; [e]134.8 × 1.2 = 161.7; [f]161.7 × 1.2 = 194.0; [g]194.0 × 1.2 = 232.9; [h]232.9 × 1.2 = 279.5; [i]279.5 × 1.2 = 334.5; [j]334.5 × 1.2 = 402.5; [k]402.5 × 1.2 = 483.0; [l]483.0 × 1.2 = 579.6; [m]579.6 × 1.2 = 695.5 (Since the maximum in the contract was 600, 600 was taken.) 600 was applied for the remaining years.

Exhibit 8: **Analysis of Swap at JPY65/AUD**

Date	Amount	Spot (JPY/AUD)	Effective Rate due to the Contract (JPY/AUD)	Profit/Loss (JPY)
1 Dec 2008	1,000,000	60	78	−18,000,000[a]
1 Jan 2009	1,000,000	60	101.4[b]	−52,400,000
1 Feb 2009	1,000,000	60	131.8[c]	−71,800,000
1 Mar 2009	1,000,000	60	171.3[d]	−111,300,000
1 Apr 2009	1,000,000	60	222.7[e]	−162,700,000
1 May 2009	1,000,000	60	289.5[f]	−229,500,000
1 Jun 2009	1,000,000	60	376.4[g]	−316,400,000
1 Jul 2009	1,000,000	60	489.2[h]	−429,200,000
1 Aug 2009	1,000,000	60	600[i]	−540,000,000
1 Sep 2009	1,000,000	60	600	−540,000,000
1 Oct 2009	1,000,000	60	600	−540,000,000
1 Nov 2009	1,000,000	60	600	−540,000,000
1 Dec 2009	1,000,000	60	600	−540,000,000
1 Jan 2010	1,000,000	60	600	−540,000,000
1 Feb 2010	1,000,000	60	600	−540,000,000
1 Mar 2010	1,000,000	60	600	−540,000,000
1 Apr 2010	1,000,000	60	600	−540,000,000
1 May 2010	1,000,000	60	600	−540,000,000
1 Jun 2010	1,000,000	60	600	−540,000,000
1 Jul 2010	1,000,000	60	600	−540,000,000
1 Aug 2010	1,000,000	60	600	−540,000,000
1 Sep 2010	1,000,000	60	600	−540,000,000
1 Oct 2010	1,000,000	60	600	−540,000,000
1 Nov 2010	1,000,000	60	600	−540,000,000
Total				−10,031,300,000

Notes: [a]$(60 \times 1,000,000) - (78 \times 1,000,000) = -18,000,000$; [b]$78 \times 78/60 = 78 \times 1.3 = 101.4$; [c]$101.4 \times 78/60 = 101.4 \times 1.3 = 131.8$; [d]$131.8 \times 1.3 = 171.3$; [e]$171.3 \times 1.3 = 222.7$; [f]$222.7 \times 1.3 = 289.5$; [g]$289.5 \times 1.3 = 376.4$; [h]$376.4 \times 1.3 = 489.2$; [i]$489.2 \times 1.3 = 636.0$ (Since the maximum in the contract was 600, 600 was taken.) 600 was applied for the remaining years.

Horino observed that Shogaki's next step was to sue BNP, as the derivative seller, for damages it suffered in accordance with relevant laws[25] in Japan. He based this decision on the assertion that BNP had breached its duty of explanation, had abused its superior bargaining position, and had inappropriately and unfairly solicited an agreement with Saizeriya.

As the seller of financial instruments in Japan, BNP needed to adhere to Japanese law; therefore it had a duty of explanation to its client, Saizeriya, in accordance with Japan's Act on Sales of Financial Instruments, Article 3(1) which stated: "When a financial instruments provider etc., intends to carry out sales etc., of financial instruments on a regular basis, it shall explain the following matters as specified below to customers at, or before, the time that the sale of financial instruments are carried out."[26] Banks also had a duty of explanation under tort liability and vicarious liability according to the Japanese Civil Code (Articles 415, 709, and 715).[27]

But the Court of First Instance in Tokyo found that BNP had not breached its responsibilities with regard to tort liability under vicarious liability related to a breach of duty of explanation, and it dismissed all claims by the company.[28]

---

[25] In Japan, there was duty of explanation for the seller of financial instruments. Japanese Act on Sales of Financial Instruments, Article 3(1) provides:

"When a Financial Instruments Provider, etc. intends to carry out Sales, etc. of Financial Instruments on a regular basis, he/she shall explain the following matters as specified below (hereinafter referred to as "Important Matters") to Customers at or before the time that the Sale of Financial Instruments, etc. is carried out."

See the Japanese Act on Sales of Financial Instruments, Article 3(1), https://liblawuw. libguides.com/c.php?g=1239338&p=9069990, accessed 3 December 2020.

Also, sophisticated institutions like banks had a duty of explanation under tort liability and vicarious liability in Japanese Civil Code, Articles 415, 709, and 715, https:// liblawuw.libguides.com/c.php?g=1239338&p=9069990, accessed 3 December 2020.

[26] *Ibid.*

[27] *Ibid.*

[28] Tokyo District Court, 28 August 2015, no. 16105. This judgment had not been made public. However, the Supreme Court allows viewing. The author visited the Supreme Court on 28 August 2016 and viewed it.

Saizeriya's management appealed that decision. The company presented its claim to the Court of Second Instance, which also denied any tort liability related to a breach of duty of explanation by BNP. It also agreed with the original ruling handed down by the Court of First Instance.[29] Saizeriya's third and final appeal to Japan's Supreme Court was also dismissed, although the court decided not to make its considerations public.[30]

A Critical Approach

Horino carefully studied the reasons why Saizeriya's cases were dismissed, in order to determine whether or not he could find a way to effectively use the same currency hedging strategy without risk to the firm.[31] In particular, he noted the following matters outlined in the court's decision-making process:

(1) BNP distributed a communication that outlined how the purpose of the swap was to secure rates for foreign currency exchange that were lower than the market rates or to hedge against the risk of foreign exchange fluctuations associated with a foreign currency-based debt. But the court questioned the extent to which the company had an adequate understanding of the details of the financial transactions.

(2) The court also questioned whether the coupon swap contracts were designed to facilitate pure hedging or whether a speculative element had been incorporated into the product. In the opinion of the court, the latter was the case. The courts questioned how much BNP should have clarified and ensured that the directional view on the exchange rate of the JPY and AUD was outlined to Saizeriya's management, based on data and knowledge it had, and whether there was any speculation by the company.

(3) Japan's courts all questioned the extent to which banks, generally, had a fiduciary responsibility (a relationship based on trust with their

---

[29]Tokyo High Court, 2012 (*ne*) No. 4820. This judgment was not made public. However, the Supreme Court allows viewing. The author visited the Supreme Court on 28 August 2016 and viewed it.

[30]Supreme Court, 2013 (*ne*) No. 1493, Shumin, No. 243, p. 51, see for the details, https://www.courts.go.jp/app/hanrei_jp/detail2?id=83047, accessed 23 November 2020.

[31]See footnotes 21, 22, and 23.

clients), which ensured the interests of their clients were protected. Although BNP sold derivatives to Saizeriya, it was also in a position to profit from those transactions. The court concluded that under Japanese law, investment banks were not bound by a fiduciary duty.

(4) Japan's Court of First Instance in Tokyo examined the extent to which BNP had adequately explained the nuances of the product in a manner that Saizeriya could have reasonably understood. Lawyers from both sides debated whether BNP had a legal responsibility to ensure that the company understood the product in sufficient depth, and knew that there was a risk of currency fluctuations in both directions. The court decided that as a provider of financial services, BNP had a duty to explain any risks associated with a contract to its client, and that included any risks that were inherent in exchange rate fluctuations, together with an estimation of the maximum loss the client faced. However, the court ruled that it was difficult to contemplate how the company would have agreed to a contract of this nature if its senior management team had been aware of the true nature of the risk it took.

(5) The Court of First Instance also examined whether there was a cancellation clause incorporated in the contracts. In this case, the coupon swap trades did not offer any mechanism by which risk control could be proactively managed, and there were no escape clauses. The court investigated whether the company was aware that the contract could not be canceled before maturity without incurring a significant fee. After reviewing these documents, Horino saw that Saizeriya had essentially entered into the swap contract, where it had not factored in risk and to which it was bound over a long duration.

(6) The Court of First Instance investigated whether BNP had specifically made Saizeriya aware that the agreement would only benefit one party and that any benefit the company was able to access would be at a loss to BNP, and that any benefit BNP accessed could only be at the loss of the company, in other words, a zero-sum. Agreements of this nature had a role in the financial system because they shifted risk to parties that had the ability and willingness to bear it, since the second party might have had a different perception of risk or a greater tolerance to it. In this case, Saizeriya essentially did not have the ability or willingness to take on such a risk.

(7) A further issue raised in the court process was whether the company was aware that there was an inherent conflict of interest between the buyer and the seller. The courts questioned whether BNP had

explained this conflict of interest to a satisfactory degree. The coupon swap dealer, in this case BNP, entered into the agreement with knowledge about foreign exchange performance and trends, the spread of interest, and other important economic facts that impacted the performance of the currencies involved. BNP also had better access to this type of data than companies. Firms like Saizeriya were not party to the same level of information.

(8) Based on their deliberations, the courts ruled that BNP had taken satisfactory steps to explain all risks to Saizeriya. Therefore, all three Japanese courts concluded that BNP had not breached its legal and regulatory responsibilities, with regard to tort liability under a breach of duty of explanation in Japan.

(9) Although an economic analysis conducted by a third party (this entity's identity was not disclosed by the court) should have played a prominent role in the process by which the courts made their decisions, it was not included in the final deliberations of the Court of First Instance and it was not made available for public analysis. However, Horino privately studied the economic analysis of the case, conducted by that third party,[32] and included it in his currency hedging investigation.

The Path Forward

After reviewing the court documents, Horino realized that before Saizeriya signed the coupon swap contracts, it should have developed a more comprehensive strategic position on the expected changes in exchange rates between the AUD and the JPY, and that position, if made, should have been based on uncertainty about exchange rate movements.

Since the company suffered losses only when the AUD plummeted to below JPY78, a level set in the contract, he believed the company had made a significant error in terms of its own predictions. If no currency swaps had been agreed, the firm would have benefited financially from the JPY's appreciation against the AUD.

Horino realized that Saizeriya had attempted to profit from future AUD/JPY exchange rates via speculation. Although the company claimed the coupon swap contracts were entered into as a means to hedge against costs, the fact that Saizeriya did so based on speculation about

---

[32] Supra note 18.

exchange rates essentially elevated the risk to higher levels. In other words, since Saizeriya selected this particular form of swap derivative, which included forecasting exchange rates, it introduced an element of uncertainty, which elevated the company's risk against the exposure to the foreign currency.

Outcomes and Analysis

If the JPY appreciated beyond the JPY78/AUD, the currency swap would have functioned as a hedge and the company would have received AUD1mn per month from BNP for the two-year term of the contract, which Saizeriya would then use to pay its Australian suppliers.

The currency swap involved the exchange of two currencies. Saizeriya paid JPY to BNP and received AUD in return. Meanwhile, BNP paid AUD to Saizeriya and received JPY in return. The company's total payoff to BNP should have been AUD24mn. This amount equated to: JPY1.872bn (AUD1mn × JPY78/AUD × 12 months × 2 years).

As such, the swap would have worked as an effective hedge for the company if the exchange rates had continued the trend of JPY depreciation against the AUD, to more than JPY78/AUD. The agreed rate of the contracts used this formula:

(1) First agreed rate JPY78/AUD.
(2) [Previous rate] × [78/The current rate] = The current agreed rate (JPY/AUD)
   Minimum = JPY78/AUD and Maximum = JPY600/AUD

Instead, what actually happened was the JPY appreciated against the AUD to levels between JPY60/AUD and JPY65/AUD by December 2008 (see Exhibit 4). Horino realized that if Shogaki had not broken the contracts, the company would have faced a significant loss.

In an unusual move, in late 2008, Shogaki publicly disclosed the terms and conditions of the currency coupon swap contracts in detail before the company commenced litigation (see Exhibit 5),[33] and Horino noticed that a crucial problem with the currency swap was a specific clause in the contract.

---

[33] Saizeriya (10 December 2008). "Notice on Potential Valuation Loss from Derivative Transactions," https://www.saizeriya.co.jp/PDF/irpdf000113.pdf, accessed 20 December 2020.

The first agreed rate was JPY78/AUD. If the JPY appreciated against the AUD, the agreed rate thereafter would be recalculated (see Exhibits 7 and 8), based on a market rate set in Japan at 10 a.m. on the first day of every month.

Using the agreed formula, if the JPY appreciated against the AUD to JPY65/AUD, the agreed rate thereafter was recalculated by BNP in the following manner:

As of 1 December 2008, the first agreed rate between the two parties was JPY78/AUD. The loss to Saizeriya was AUD1mn × (JPY65 − JPY78) = JPY−13mn.

Based on a monthly calculation, as of 1 January 2009, the agreed rate recalculation of JPY78 × 78/65 = 78 × 1.2 = JPY93.6mn. The company's loss was calculated as follows: AUD1mn × (93.6 − 65) = JPY−28.6mn (see Exhibit 7).

If the loss continued over the two-year term of the contract (to 1 November 2010), it would have reached JPY8.727bn (see Exhibit 7).

If the exchange rate of JPY65/AUD continued for two years, Horino saw that the effective exchange rates, which determined the company's payoff amount to BNP, were as follows:

1 Dec 2008	78 × 78/65 = 78 × 1.2 = JPY93.6/AUD
1 Jan 2009	93.6 × 78/65 = 93.6 × 1.2 = 112.3
1 Feb 2009	112.3 × 1.2 = 134.8
1 Mar 2009	134.8 × 1.2 = 161.7
1 Apr 2009	161.7 × 1.2 = 194.0
1 May 2009	194.0 × 1.2 = 232.9
1 Jun 2009	232.9 × 1.2 = 279.5
1 Jul 2009	279.5 × 1.2 = 334.5
1 Aug 2009	334.5 × 1.2 = 402.5
1 Sep 2009	402.5 × 1.2 = 483.0
1 Oct 2009	483.0 × 1.2 = 579.6
1 Nov 2009–1 Nov 2010	600 (the maximum)

These extremely high effective rates were applied to the contract. If the JPY65/AUD rate continued for the two-year contracts, the company would have incurred substantial losses of JPY8.727bn and the total payoff amount, including JPY payment for the account payable of AUD1mn, to BNP was JPY10.031bn.

If the rate of JPY60/AUD continued for two years, the company incurred substantial losses of JPY10.0313bn and the payoff amount to BNP was JPY11.471bn (see Exhibits 7–10).

Shogaki and Saizeriya's board decided that these effective rates became too expensive for a foreign currency swap where the underlying transaction of the currency swap was the exchange of AUD1mn and the equivalent JPY amount, at the market rate.

The currency swap contract was settled through cash payments of profits or losses based on the above formula, where the value of the derivative part was dependent on the value of the underlying asset at a specific point in time before the expiration date on 1 April 2010.

A deliberate design feature of this currency swap was to include JPY cash payments (A), the profit and loss between the buyer and the seller (B), and the final settlement as payoff (C) as per the following:

JPY for Account Payable (A) = Monthly JPY paid for two years by Saizeriya to BNP for AUD1mn of accounts payable payment, based on the current spot rate.

at JPY60/AUD   AUD1mn × 24 months × JPY60/AUD = JPY1.440bn
    P/L Due to Swap (B) = Profit/Loss due to Swap (For payment, this shows plus number).
at JPY60/AUD   JPY10.031bn
Payoff (C = A + B) = Payoff amount of JPY by Saizeriya to BNP for AUD1mn for two years.
at JPY60/AUD   JPY(1.440b + 10.031bn) = JPY1.147bn

Exhibit 9: Agreed Rates due to the Swap Contract Based on JPY65/AUD as the Spot

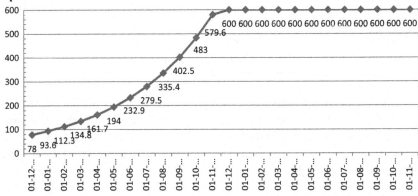

Exhibit 10:   JPY for Accounts Payable (a), P/L due to Swap (b), and Payoff (c) for AUD1M/Month for Years, 1 December 2008–1 November 2010 Unit JPY1M

	JPY for Account Payable (A)[1]	P/L due to Swap (B)[2]	Payoff (C = A + B)[3]
At JPY60/AUD	1,440[4]	10,031	11,471[5]
At JPY65/AUD	1,560	8,727	10,287
At JPY78/AUD	1,872	0	1,872
At JPY88/AUD	2,112	−240	1,872
At JPY110/AUD	2,640	−768	1,872
At JPY120/AUD	2,880	−1,008	1,872

Notes: (1) A = Monthly JPY Paid by Saizeriya to BNP Paribas for AUD1mn of Account Payable Payment, Based on the Current Spot Rate.
(2) B = Profit/Loss due to Swap.
(3) C = A + B = Payoff by Saizeriya to BNP Paribas for AUD1mn.
(4) AUD1mn × 24 months × JPY60/AUD = JPY1,440mn.
(5) JPY1,440mn + JPY10,031mn = JPY11,471mn.

Payoff is the total amount of JPY to be paid by Saizeriya to BNP for AUD1mn for two years at JPY60/AUD. The details are shown in Exhibit 10, which is a sensitivity analysis from JPY60/AUD to JPY120/AUD.

Saizeriya versus BNP Paribas

When Shogaki terminated Saizeriya's contracts with BNP and released the details of its contracts with BNP, many of the company's directors and shareholders questioned this move on the basis that he had revealed more information than the company was legally required to do.

Shogaki's decision to terminate the contracts cost the company JPY15bn, but he believed that decision saved the firm from further losses, bankruptcy, or the need to sell assets.

When Saizeriya sued the international banking group, the public became aware of the financial losses the company suffered as a result of its derivative contracts. As a result, its share price fell sharply. Before its disclosure on 21 November 2008, the company's share price was JPY2080 per share, but after that announcement, it fell to JPY801 per share — less than half its previous price.[34] Such a dramatic change high-lighted shareholder concerns about the company's future.

Even though the initial public reaction was negative, Shogaki believed that the company's stakeholders would ultimately value management's openness and transparency. Horino noticed that the former president also instigated legal action as an important ethical move, to warn other companies of the risks associated with derivatives contracts that involved forward hedging.

Although the Japanese legal system exonerated BNP, Shogaki, who retained his role as board chairman, again questioned the Japanese courts' decision in 2015. He asked why BNP was not held accountable for failing to act in its clients' best interest. He even considered suing BNP in London because he believed the company would get a better result under UK laws.

Next, Horino's explored the reasons why the former president thought legal action would be successful in the UK and had contemplated suing the London branch of BNP Paribas because the foreign currency coupon swaps originated within its London branch, before BNP Tokyo offered them to Saizeriya. He noted that Shogaki believed there was a potential course of action available to Saizeriya in the UK, as it was a common law jurisdiction. Shogaki thought UK courts would handle the case differently from Japanese courts, which were governed by statutory law.

Although Shogaki believed it would get a better result in the UK, he decided not to pursue legal action when shareholders and directors failed to agree with that move.

Decision Time

By November 2020, Horino needed to decide whether or not to undertake further currency hedging. After he analyzed the company's previous use of derivatives, Horino concluded that the financial tool had failed because of the immaturity of corporate governance systems within Saizeriya, which allowed the company's then-president Shogaki to make that decision on his own.

Horino also decided that the company's middle management lacked both the knowledge and understanding about the risks the company had

---

[34]Saizeriya (28 November 2008). "Annual Report 36th," https://www.saizeriya.co.jp/PDF/irpdf000131.pdf, accessed 31 December 2020.

faced, which meant they were unable to provide critical advice and support to Shogaki in the decision-making process.

Horino knew the company still had vital AUD-denominated accounts payable and needed to make AUD payments. Additionally, the JPY had continued to depreciate against the AUD since March 2020, which coincided with growing impact of COVID-19 in Japan. He was worried that the JPY would continue to fall, a development that would significantly affect the company's financial conditions. Given these circumstances, he needed to decide whether or not to hedge against this apparent risk, even though the previous currency swap contracts resulted in considerable losses.

The three issues associated with the use of currency swap contracts were as follows:

- They were inherently complicated and difficult to understand.
- They were subject to market and liquidity risks.
- They were often mistakenly perceived to be safe because they were managed by reputable institutions such as banks.

Horino knew that effective management involved Saizeriya taking positive action to offset currency risks. He realized that the company would be unable to profit from the currency swap if the JPY appreciated against the AUD, and he also understood that failure to hedge and hedging were both accompanied by risks because the company had a portfolio of negative and positive cash flows that were both directly impacted by exchange rate performance.

He was also aware that some companies opted to leave currency risk exposures unhedged on the basis that such exposures were an acknowledged part of business activities and that currency netted in a portfolio of negative and positive cash flows would eventually correct any changes in the value of the currencies held.

His own experience taught him that companies should not develop hedging strategies without first clearly delineating the currency movement expectations. Having set expectations out in this way, the company should choose to hedge risk only if other strategies and options were fully evaluated. He believed derivative users should be shrewd enough to identify the best financial instrument through which the risk and utility function of a company were met. He noted that Saizeriya's past dealings with BNP highlighted the need to ensure that management executives were

Exhibit 11:   Saizeriya's Stock Prices for 2016–2020

Source: Yahoo! Finance Stock Prices, http://finance.yahoo.com/, accessed 28 November 2020.

aware of the risks and benefits associated with a financial agreement before any formal agreement was reached.

As part of his deliberations, Horino also considered whether stakeholders, i.e., shareholders and lending banks, wanted Saizeriya's management to hedge against currency risk or whether they preferred to offset risk by purchasing alternative securities. Saizeriya needed to consider its stakeholders because the company's stock prices declined significantly during the Covid-19 pandemic (see Exhibit 11), a movement Horino knew indicated that those stakeholders were not happy with the company's financial outlook.

After careful analysis of Saizeriya's previous hedging experience, Horino formed an option that solid corporate governance policies and procedures were required for hedging to be successful. Although processes had previously been in place within the company, they failed in their fundamental objectives of protection against risk. He was also concerned about the attitude that some members of the management team exhibited toward corporate governance.

He analyzed the corporate governance systems in place at the company and he identified the following areas that needed to be reviewed:

(1) Although a degree of risk-taking was essential to the ongoing progress of the business, the costs associated with risks were significantly underestimated, from both internal and external perspectives. In addition, cost incurred in terms of management time required to rectify this situation had also been underestimated. He realized that a corporate governance model was required that could identify, manage, and mitigate risks within the business.

(2) Financial risk governance standards within Saizeriya were focused on internal control and audits, and did not adequately consider *ex ante* identification or the ongoing management of risk. A corporate governance approach that placed an emphasis on *ex ante* identification of risks needed to be developed.

(3) Risk governance standards within the company tended to operate at a very high level; this limited their practical everyday usefulness. Horino saw there was an opportunity to implement more operational and practical risk governance standards that could be applied across a range of different situations.

(4) Horino realized that Saizeriya's board failed to pay attention to potentially catastrophic risks associated with the use of derivatives. While these were unlikely to occur, there was still a distinct requirement to manage them. Any risks with the potential to have a major impact on the business and its stakeholders needed to be given due attention by the board.

(5) Horino recognized that the board's members needed to have greater knowledge and understanding about the drawbacks related to risk management models within the company, especially those that relied on debatable probability assumptions.

(6) He believed potential new board members needed to be better screened to ensure all members had sufficient knowledge and understanding of the risks associated with investment decisions made by the board.

(7) There was also a need to achieve a better balance between risk controlled through direction from the ownership function and that delegated to the board of directors. This was also reflected in the balance between risk-taking control through top-down rules and control that placed a high degree of reliance on boards.

(8) The relevant ownership function should take every opportunity, in both regular ownership dialogue and when formulating strategic directives, to ensure that the company had robust risk management frameworks in place.

Horino understood the company needed a solid corporate governance model that operated in the best interests of the organization and stakeholders, to ensure informed decisions about risk were made based on accurate and comprehensive information. He believed risk management remained the primary responsibility of line managers, once robust corporate governance frameworks were used.

As a result of his thorough analysis, Horino decided to form risk management teams at the middle-management level, as it was these employees who were responsible for tracking derivative transactions in advance of trading to ensure all corporate regulations, strategies, and requirements were met and adhered to. He also put in place processes to guarantee that all existing agreements were strictly monitored, and action was taken immediately to offset any risks when they became apparent.

Saizeriya's president Issei Horino decided to submit these suggestions to his next board meeting for action.

For Further Discussion

(1) On 9 December 2008, Shogaki announced the company had incurred losses as a result of its foreign currency coupon swaps, and he also disclosed the full details of this derivative to the public. Some of company's directors and shareholders questioned his actions. The company's stock price fell following the disclosure. Although Japanese laws are not clear regarding what is subject to disclosure, Shogaki was confident that he had done the right thing, and he believed that shareholders would eventually appreciate the company's transparency. When are companies in Japan, e.g., Saizeriya's management, required to disclose and how much are they required to reveal?

(2) Evaluate the role economic analysis played in the Japanese court decisions related to this derivative case.

(3) The company filed civil suits against BNP with the Tokyo District Court on 3 July 2012 seeking damages of JPY16.8bn. Some directors and shareholders questioned the decision to file a civil suit. But then president Shogaki felt confident that he was doing the right thing and that the shareholders would appreciate his decision, regardless of whether the company won or lost its case. Evaluate his decision.

(4) Hedging exchange risk is a strategy that can be used during periods of unusual currency volatility. What is hedging? Why do companies hedge? What were the pros and cons of hedging?

(5) Shogaki was not happy with the outcome of the court cases. He questioned why investment banks were not required to act in their clients' best interests? How would you answer this question?

(6) After his civil suits failed, Shogaki considered suing BNP in London. He was aware that the foreign currency coupon swaps had originated in the London branch of BNP before its Tokyo branch offered them to Saizeriya. As the UK is a common law jurisdiction, he hoped that the UK courts would handle the case differently than the Japanese courts, which were governed by statutory law. Since the company's actions in Japanese courts had failed, he hoped Saizeriya would get a better result elsewhere. Would the company get a better result under UK laws?

(7) The company's current president, Horino, supports good corporate governance as a way to ensure hedging is successful. Comment on his decision.

Case 7

Bank of Japan's Dilemma: Should Its Ultra-easy Monetary Policy End Under Inflationary Pressure and a Weak JPY?*

On 8 June 2022, Japan's currency (JPY) fell to its lowest level in almost six years due to a combination of the Bank of Japan's (BOJ) ultra-loose monetary policy and a series of rate hikes by the US Federal Reserve.

As Japan's currency dropped to JPY134.42 to the US dollar (USD), import costs increased, exacerbated by rising commodities prices for resources such as copper, aluminum, and wheat. Earlier that year, global concerns over supply after Russia's invasion of Ukraine pushed US crude oil futures to USD130 per barrel, the highest level since 2008.

---

*This case was prepared by Professor Mitsuru Misawa. Dr Misawa is a Professor of Finance and Director of the Centre for Japanese Global Investment and Finance at the University of Hawaii at Manoa. During his time as an executive officer at the Industrial Bank of Japan (now Mizuho Corporate Bank), Dr Misawa acted as an international investment banker in charge of various industries in Japan.

This case is Part 4 of a four-part case series about the Bank of Japan. It may be taught on a stand-alone basis or combined with the other cases to create a joint-negotiation exercise.

This case is not intended to show effective or ineffective handling of decision-making or business processes. The author might have disguised certain information to protect confidentiality. Cases are written in the past tense, this is not meant to imply that all practices, organizations, people, places, or facts mentioned in the case no longer occur, exist, or apply.

Haruhiko Kuroda,[1] the Governor of the Bank of Japan, repeatedly stated that a weak JPY benefited the nation's economy. However, a weaker domestic currency resulted in higher prices for petroleum, cereals, and imported goods, which adversely impacted businesses and the local population.

The bank faced a difficult situation. If fiscal spending was increased in response to commodity price rises, it risked further undermining the currency. Japan's government had already lifted the threshold on subsidies to oil wholesalers, which, if increased, further weakened the JPY.

As the JPY fell, the BOJ responded with massive purchases of risky assets and long-term government bonds, a move that reflected its aim of a 2% price-stability inflation target.[2] But efforts to re-energize the nation's economy needed to be handled carefully because the BOJ had to be wary of any negative consequences. It needed to be flexible to avoid exceeding the inflation target, and diligent in its purchases of government bonds to preclude that measure from being misinterpreted as an effort to repair Japan's massive budget shortfall.

However, the government's increased spending to take advantage of historically low interest rates weakened the nation's fiscal discipline. Was it time to call a halt to aggressive monetary easing by the BOJ?

Abenomics and Japan's Currency

The JPY's attraction was based on Japan's position as the world's largest net creditor economy. Before the 2008 financial crisis, the JPY and Swiss franc were popular borrowing currencies because of their historically low interest rates.

In the quarter following the September 2008 financial crisis, the JPY strengthened from JPY106 to JPY88 against the USD, and in the three months after the March 2011 earthquake and tsunami, the currency appreciated from around JPY83 to JPY80.

Four months after Shinzo Abe became Prime Minister in December 2012, the Japanese parliament appointed Kuroda as the Governor of the

---

[1]Bank of Japan, "Governor [The 31st]: Mr KURODA Haruhiko," https://www.forbes.com/profile/haruhiko-kuroda/?sh=4effd4052136, accessed 21 June 2022.

[2]M. Misawa (2006). "Bank of Japan's Meeting in March 2006: An End to the Quantitative Easing Policy?" Asia Case Research Centre, The University of Hong Kong, Ref. 06/301C.

Bank of Japan.[3] In the eight years that he held office, Abe promoted three economic stimulus goals — known as the three arrows in the Prime Minister's quiver — economic growth, monetary easing, and fiscal reform. These economic policies were called "Abenomics."[4]

Abenomics combined monetary relaxation and heavy fiscal spending with targeted growth strategies. It included a target of 2% annual inflation to correct excessive JPY appreciation, radical quantitative easing, expanded public investment, and increased buying of Japanese Government Bonds (JGB) by the BOJ (see Appendix 1).

Abenomics in Action

On the day that Kuroda was appointed as the BOJ's new governor, he announced a plan that doubled the bank's monetary base for the next two years, primarily through increased JGB buying (see Appendices 2 and 3). He intended to establish Abe's target of a 2% annual rate of inflation in the first round of the Prime Minister's policy push, and to induce the wealth effect with aggressive easy-money strategies. He also wanted to encourage real demand that buoyed corporate investment and consumer spending so that Japan could overcome 20 years of deflation (see Appendices 4 and 5).

On 4 April 2013, the bank's policy board met and adopted nearly all of Kuroda's proposals. It endorsed the 2% price-rise target, with a time horizon of about two years. Even before that meeting, Kuroda told BOJ employees that half measures would not work. He rejected suggestions to incrementally ramp up easing, after he weighed the benefits and risks of each step. By taking every conceivable measure at the same time, he drove home the point that the central bank's monetary easing had entered a new dimension.[5] The BOJ's aggressive easing program and Kuroda's bold strategy surprised financial markets.

The bank's new policy played on the word "double" — double the monetary base and double the purchases of government bonds and

---

[3] M. Misawa, "Bank of Japan's Meeting in March 2006."

[4] M. Misawa (2013). "Abenomics of Japan: What Was It: Could This Conquer Japan's Decade-Long Deflation?" Harvard Business School Case, Harvard Business Publishing, HKU1017, vol. 13/534C.

[5] M. Misawa (2020). "Negative Interest Rates: The Bank of Japan Experience," Harvard Business School Case, Harvard Business Publishing, HKU1235, vol. 20/651C.

exchange-traded funds. The emphasis on "double" also sent a message to markets that the BOJ was a bolder and more active central bank. As the bank planned to end money easing in two years, the markets named this the BOJ "2–2–2" policy.

The bank's monetary base consisted of financial institutions' current-account deposits and cash circulating in the market. It expanded this base with increased purchases of JGB holdings. It also expected that the increased funds in the current-account deposits would eventually find their way into businesses and households.

The BOJ planned to guide financial markets so that monetary supply grew by JPY60–70tn a year. This meant Japan's monetary base, which stood at JPY138tn at the end of 2012, climbed to JPY200tn by the end of 2013, and JPY270tn a year later.

The BOJ also expanded the scope of government debt purchases to all JGB, and included the longest 40-year instruments.

The bank's previous governor, Masaaki Shirakawa, had lowered interest rates on bonds maturing in one to three years. But Kuroda extended the average remaining maturity of the bank's JGB holdings from slightly less than three years to roughly seven years. The new policy's qualitative aspect had to do with the fact that the BOJ planned to push down long-term interest rates by buying more bonds with longer terms to maturity. By bringing down long-term rates, the BOJ hoped to encourage individuals to take out mortgages and businesses to make capital investments.

The bank also boosted holdings of exchange-traded funds by JPY1tn a year and bought real estate investment trusts. It hoped these would raise stock and property prices and create a wealth effect that spurred consumer spending and business investments.

Growth of Market Concerns

The BOJ's decision to pursue an ultra-loose monetary policy caused concern in the markets.[6] The largest concern was a rise in consumption of foreign energy that resulted from having most of the nation's nuclear power plants off-line. Energy imports increased by several trillion JPY a year compared to those before the March 2011 Tohoku natural disaster,[7] and as the JPY softened further, this increased in value terms. In turn,

---

[6] *Ibid.*
[7] *Ibid.*

Japan's trade deficits became chronic, and its current-account surplus decreased. On the upside, a weak JPY bolstered exports.

At first, stocks of property developers and financial institutions, which were bought aggressively, boosted the Tokyo stock market. The JPY's fall prompted the purchase of blue-chip exporters, which hit a year-to-date high in 2022. Because of lower interest rates, investment money flew into the stock market. Investors expected the banks' bold monetary easing to spur further rises in share prices,[8] and the BOJ plan to increase purchases of risky assets fueled hopes for still higher stock and real estate prices. But investors were worried about how long this trend would continue.

The outlook for the government bond market appeared uncertain. The 10-year yield swung as market participants digested the BOJ plan to buy more than JPY7tn of bonds every month. The BOJ's purchases could have decreased trading in Japan. Investor concerns about the volume of bonds circulating in the market as a result of the bank purchases might have resulted in these investors leaving the domestic bond market.

By ensuring the JPY stayed weak, the BOJ expected firms to respond accordingly. Since the market moved in the direction the bank wanted, it looked for changes in corporate outlooks for investment and earnings. Recognition grew that the JPY had weakened over the long term. A weaker JPY potentially enhanced the export competitiveness of Japanese manufacturers and helped to stimulate consumer spending. But investors were concerned about how long this positive trend would continue.

Companies were not convinced by the currency's dramatic depreciation after November 2012. A survey[9] in March 2013, when the JPY–USD rate was in the mid-90s, showed that large manufacturers forecast a rate of only a little more than JPY85 for the fiscal year 2013, and they subsequently adopted a cautious outlook for the future.

Kuroda's pressure on the BOJ to further ease its monetary policy did have some beneficial impact on the markets. A weaker JPY enhanced the national gross domestic product (GDP), and left Japan's corporate sector with record earnings. What it didn't do was incentivize chief executive officers to raise workers' wages. It also didn't encourage business leaders to invest in innovation, enhance their company's productivity, or take

---

[8] *Ibid.*

[9] Cabinet Office, "Monthly Economic Report," June 2013, https://www5.cao.go.jp/keizai3/getsurei-e/2013jun.html, accessed 10 July 2022.

risks in innovative disruption. In fact, only one key measure was fully utilized — the BOJ's monetary strategy of additional easing.

What Happened Next

When Kuroda accelerated the BOJ ultra-loose monetary policy, he ignored the risks associated with rapid monetary easing and instead focused on meeting the 2% inflation target. To stress his commitment to the policy, Kuroda stated that it was inappropriate to develop an exit strategy from substantial monetary easing.

Kuroda rapidly extended the bank's balance sheet, which by 2018 surpassed the size of the nation's USD5tn GDP. Japan caught up with advanced countries pushing unrestricted credit to extremes after a fragmented and somewhat tokenistic drive for monetary easing. This fundamentally altered Japan's position in relation to Europe, the US, and emerging economies.

However, there were indications that monetary easing had not provided the economic support the BOJ wanted.[10] After nine years of flooding Japan with JPY, consumer prices only approached the 2% targeted inflation in April 2022, but "bad" inflation was imported via surging energy and commodity prices, as the Ukraine–Russia crisis exacerbated the COVID-19 pandemic's disruptions to global supply chains.

By January 2022, the nation's growing trade imbalance resulted in Japan's current-account deficit reaching JPY1.19tn (USD10.1bn), the second highest on record. At the same time Japan's exports fell, and there were fewer purchases of JPY that were converted to foreign-currency profits as more Japanese firms expanded their overseas operations. While international businesses generated more money for firms, these were typically recorded in the original currency. If Japan's account value remained negative, its large net foreign assets diminished.[11]

The JPY carry trade, which contributed to the trend of JPY buying in uncertain times, also halted. Currency traders borrowed low-interest currencies to invest in higher-yielding currencies or other market assets that offered higher rates. Borrowed currencies tended to appreciate when

[10]*Ibid.*

[11]S. Otsuka (30 March 2022). "Yen at Risk of Downward Spiral Fueled by Trade Deficit, BOJ Easing," *Nikkei Asia*, https://asia.nikkei.com/Economy/Yen-at-risk-of-downward-spiral-fueled-by-trade-deficit-BOJ-easing, accessed 28 May 2022.

market conditions deteriorated as investors reversed their holdings. Borrowing in USD increased in popularity as the US Federal Reserve slashed interest rates to near-zero levels.

As the US Federal Reserve moved closer to raising rates, traders' attention returned to the JPY, and the carry trade's initial borrowing phase to convert JPY to USD pushed the JPY even lower. Markets were now more concerned about Japanese stagflation than with the nation's economy's recovery.

No Longer a Secure Refuge

The once-dominant JPY was no longer a secure refuge. The currency declined more than other prominent currencies as the global economy responded to Russia's invasion of Ukraine — a signal that the JPY had also declined in appeal as a safe-haven currency in times of crisis.

As Japan shifted away from the export-heavy economy that fueled investors' attraction to the JPY during conflicts, pandemics, and other crises, high resource prices had a greater impact on its current-account balance. As the nation's current-account deficit grew wider, fears increased that a weaker JPY would plunge the currency into a negative spiral (see Exhibit 1).

Exhibit 1: Current Balance, Japan

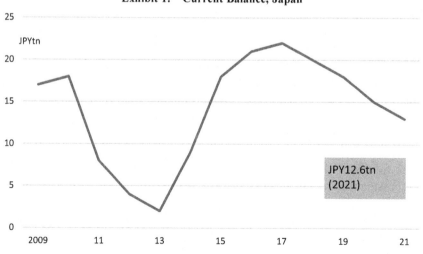

Source: The Bank of Japan, Home, Statistics, https://www.boj.or.jp/en/statistics/index.htm/, accessed 22 May 2022).

The BOJ attempted to defend its ultra-loose monetary policy on 28 March 2022, when it conducted bond-buying operations that drove the JPY to a seven-year low. When it decided to keep the 10-year JGB benchmark yield below its 0.25% target, the BOJ went against a global trend as other central banks raised interest rates to combat inflation.

Kuroda's strategy exacerbated the JPY's depreciation, aggravated Japan's current-account deficit in the balance of payments, and accelerated inflation.

Although the US Federal Reserve initially kept rates at low levels, other central banks shifted in the opposite direction. As a result, interest rate differentials widened, and the JPY fell. This added further pressure on Japanese firms and local consumers, particularly when increased commodity prices were taken into account.

In response to growing inflationary pressures, the US Federal Reserve raised its benchmark rate on 30 March 2022 after keeping it near zero for two years. A day later, the Bank of England also raised interest rates for the third time since December 2021. Despite the inflationary outlook, the BOJ remained committed to monetary easing.

When Japan and US Rates Cross

The BOJ's struggle against rising interest rates accelerated the JPY's depreciation, which was attributed to the growing interest rate gap between Japan and the US (see Exhibit 2). The effect of the monetary policy divergence between Japan and the US became clearer when the real interest rate, after deduction of the price forecast, was examined. In March 2022, the real interest rates in Japan and the US crossed. The rate in the US rose, while the rate in Japan fell. For the first time since March 2020, when the COVID-19 pandemic spread globally, the US real interest rate overtook Japan. This created a powerful JPY-selling machine (see Exhibits 3 and 4).

Even after the loss of principal value due to inflation, positive returns were forecast, which made US Treasury bonds even more tempting. The circumstances in which JGB were expected to return less than price increases had deteriorated, which lowered their net value. The difference in real interest rates between Japan and the US reached an important benchmark (see Exhibit 4).

Exhibit 2: USD/JPY (1980–2022)

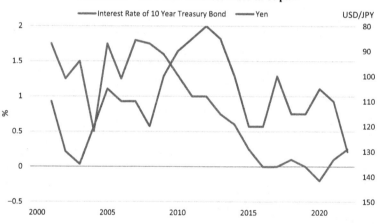

Source: The Bank of Japan, Home, Statistics, https://www.boj.or.jp/en/statistics/index.htm/, accessed 22 May 2022).

Exhibit 3: JPY and Interest Rate in Japan

Source: The Bank of Japan, Home, Statistics, https://www.boj.or.jp/en/statistics/index.htm/, accessed 22 May 2022.

It was an ideal environment for investors, as short-term gains for JPY carry transactions were predicted with great accuracy. Investors bought USD and borrowed JPY at a real negative rate of interest. As a result of these carry transactions, the JPY depreciated even more.

Exhibit 4:　Real Interest Rates between US and Japan (Yields of 10-Year Price-Linked Treasury Bonds)

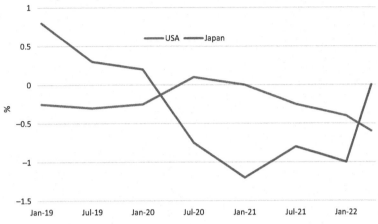

Source: The Bank of Japan, Home, Statistics, https://www.boj.or.jp/en/statistics/index.htm/, accessed 22 May 2022.

Japan and the US agreed to work together. On 29 March 2022, Japan's top currency diplomat and Vice Finance Minister for International Affairs, Masato Kanda, and his US counterpart, Andy Baukol, the acting Under Secretary of International Affairs at the US Department of Treasury, agreed that monetary authorities in both countries would communicate closely on currency issues. Kanda said: "Exchange rate stability is important and rapid fluctuations are undesirable. We will closely monitor developments in the foreign exchange market and their impact on the Japanese economy with a firm sense of urgency, including the recent depreciation of the JPY."[12] On 30 March 2022, Prime Minister Fumio Kishida met the BOJ's governor in Tokyo,[13] but on 1 April 2022, Kuroda stated: "It was not necessary or appropriate to tighten our monetary policy."[14]

---

[12]"Japan, U.S. to Communicate Closely on Forex Issues After Yen Slides," *Nikkei Asia*, 29 March 2022, https://asia.nikkei.com/Business/Markets/Japan-U.S.-to-communicate-closely-on-forex-issues-after-yen-slides, accessed 11 May 2022.

[13]"Yen Surges to 121-Level as BOJ Governor Meets with Kishida," *Nikkei Asia*, 30 March 2022, https://asia.nikkei.com/Business/Markets/Currencies/Yen-surges-to-121-level-as-BOJ-governor-meets-Kishida, accessed 11 May 2022.

[14]T. Gakuto (30 March 2022). "BOJ's Lone Battle against Rising Yields Accelerates Yen's Slide," *Nikkei Asia*, https://asia.nikkei.com/Business/Markets/Currencies/BOJ-s-lone-battle-against-rising-yields-accelerates-yen-s-slide, accessed 28 May 2022.

Three weeks later, Japan's Finance Minister, Shunichi Suzuki, and the US Secretary of the Treasury, Janet Yellen, met after a gathering of international finance chiefs at the Group of 20 (G20) meeting in Washington, DC. They also agreed to closely communicate on currency movements in response to the JPY's recent rapid decline to a 20-year low against the USD. After their meeting, Suzuki said: "The currency's rapid fluctuations are undesirable, but the movements are fast indeed. We have to monitor the developments with vigilance."[15]

Decision Time: Should the BOJ End Monetary Easing?

In countering the threat of broader monetary policy divergence between the two nations, the JPY sank sharply against the USD. Although the BOJ continued with vigorous monetary easing, the US Federal Reserve started to restrict its monetary policy as inflation rose.

Japanese exporters viewed a weak JPY as a bonus when funds were repatriated because it improved their overseas profits. But when coupled with an increased cost of crude oil and other commodities, it raised import costs and hindered consumer spending in Japan, a resource-scarce economy.

The bank's decision to raise government bond purchases made it more difficult to end its policy of monetary easing. If the economy escaped deflation and interest rates rose, the BOJ needed to be concerned about sustaining big losses. The BOJ might need to determine that a greater emphasis on the financial system should be factored in when it ended its ultra-loose monetary policy in the future, as higher bond yields at lower prices could imperil the financial soundness of the BOJ and private investment firms.

Long rates could rise if budgetary discipline deteriorated, resulting in a loss of market confidence. The BOJ acquisition of longer-term bonds also made ending monetary easing difficult. If the bank's 2% inflation target was met and it sold its JGB holdings, the chance that it would incur losses increased significantly. Would the depreciation of the JPY be

---

[15]"Japan, U.S. to Communicate Amid Yen's Rapid Fall," *Nikkei Asia*, 22 April 2022, https://asia.nikkei.com/Business/Markets/Currencies/Japan-U.S.-agree-to-closely-communicate-amid-yen-s-rapid-fall, accessed 11 May 2022.

stemmed by a more accommodating monetary policy? Or was that likely to threaten Japan's public finances?

One of the most important indicators of fiscal health was the national debt-to-GDP ratio. The US had a high of 133% in 2021, while the UK had a low of 108%. But Japan had a high of 256%. Even if the balance between long- and short-term government bonds increased by JPY280tn over the past decade, Japan's interest rates failed to increase since the BOJ accumulated JPY460tn in government bond holdings. However, the bank's more accommodating monetary policy had succeeded in bridging the demand–supply gap in government borrowing.

Japan's finances were vulnerable to interest rate rises due to the massive debt held by the state. The Ministry of Finance claimed that the cost of principal and interest payments in FY2023 would climb by JPY3.7tn if interest rates increased by 1% during that time. The quandary of obtaining that sum of money persisted when Japan's budget for fiscal 2022 was JPY1076tn (see Exhibit 5).

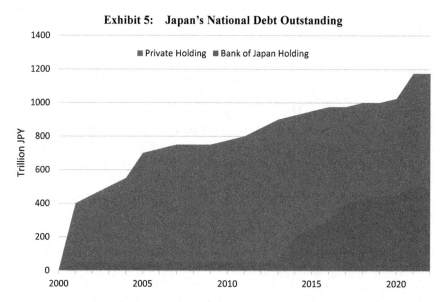

Exhibit 5:   Japan's National Debt Outstanding

Source: The Bank of Japan, Home, Statistics, https://www.boj.or.jp/en/statistics/index.htm/, accessed 22 May 2022.

But what action could Japan's Prime Minister, Fumio Kishida, take to stop the JPY's decline?[16] The first step was to admit that Japan's fixation with a weakened JPY caused terrible repercussions. A major concern was how Abenomics' decade-long focus on weaker currency levels had harmed Japan's economic muscle and capacities.

Kuroda emphasized that the BOJ would retain its current policy if an increase in the consumer price index seemed temporary and not sustained. He cautioned that if the index rose above 2%, the BOJ would change its policies. Kuroda's term of office as Governor of the Bank of Japan was scheduled to end in April 2023, but with an Upper House election in 2022, he was under domestic pressure to ensure that inflation remained under control.

Appendix 1: International Party Conditions in Equilibrium: Related Formulas[17]

Suppose:

S = the spot exchange rate (a direct quote on JPY is, e.g., JPY/USD) at the beginning of the period (S_1) and the end of the period (S_2)

I^{JPY} = the Japanese interest rate

I^{USD} = the US interest rate

π^{JPY} = inflation risk

π^{USD} = inflation risk

Home currency = JPY

(1) Δ% *Change in S*

In direct quotation when the home currency price for a foreign currency is used, the formula becomes

---

[16]"Japan, U.S. to Communicate Closely on Forex Issues After Yen Slides," *Nikkei Asia*, 29 March 2022, https://asia.nikkei.com/Business/Markets/Japan-U.S.-to-communicate-closely-on-forex-issues-after-yen-slides, accessed 22 May 2022.

[17]D.K. Eiteman, A.I. Stonehill, and M.H. Moffett (2013). *Multinational Business Finance*, 13th edn. (New York: Pearson Series in Finance).

$$\Delta\% \text{ Change} = \frac{(S_2 - S_1)}{S_1}$$

(2) *Purchasing Power Parity (PPP)*

According to the relative PPP, the relative change in prices between two countries over a period of time determines the change in the exchange rate over that period. The formula becomes

$$S_2 = S_1 \times \frac{1 + \pi^{\text{Yen}}}{1 + \pi^{\text{USD}}}$$

The following figure shows a general case of relative PPP. The vertical axis shows the % change in S for foreign currency, and the horizontal axis shows the % difference in rates of inflation (foreign relative to home country). The diagonal parity line shows the equilibrium position between a change in the exchange rate and inflation rates.

Relative Purchasing Power Parity (PPP)

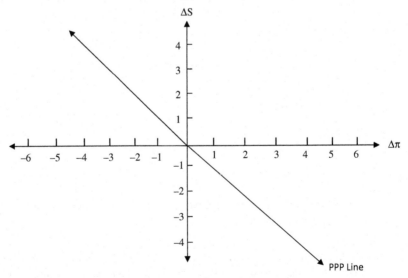

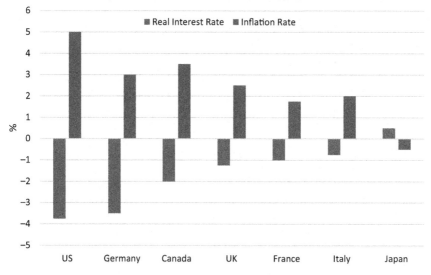

Exhibit 6: The International Fisher Effect

Note: $r = i - \pi$.

Source: The Bank of Japan, Home, Statistics, https://www.boj.or.jp/en/statistics/index.htm/, accessed 22 May 2022.

(3) *The International Fisher Effect*

The forecast change in the spot exchange rate is equal to, but opposite in sign to, the differential between nominal interest rates. The relationship between the percentage change in S over time and the differential between interest rates in different markets is known as the international Fisher Effect (see Exhibit 6).

The formula becomes

$$\frac{(S_2 - S_1)}{S_1} = (i^{\text{Yen}} - i^{\text{USD}})$$

(4) *The Fisher Effect*

The real rate of return (r) is the nominal rate of interest (i) less the expected rate of inflation (π). Assuming efficient and open markets, the real rates of return should be equal across currencies.

The formula is $r = i - \pi$.

(5) *Prices, Interest Rates, and Exchange Rates in Equilibrium*

The following figure illustrates all of the fundamental parity relations in equilibrium, using the USD and JPY.

International Party Conditions in Equilibrium

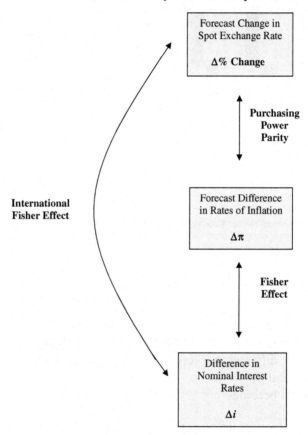

Appendix 2: The BOJ's Mission Statement

The Bank of Japan (BOJ) is the central bank of Japan. It is a juridical body based on the Bank of Japan Act,[18] and is not a government agency or a private corporation.

---

[18] Bank of Japan Act (Act No. 89 of 18 June 1997), https://www.boj.or.jp/en/about/outline/data/foboj12.pdf, accessed 21 June 2022.

The Law states the BOJ's objectives are to issue banknotes, to carry out currency and monetary control, and to ensure smooth settlement of funds among banks and other financial institutions, thereby contributing to the maintenance of an orderly financial system. It also stipulates the BOJ's principle of currency and monetary control as follows: Currency and monetary control shall be aimed at, through the pursuit of price stability, contributing to the sound development of the national economy.

According to its charter, the missions of the BOJ are as follows:

- Issuance and management of banknotes,
- Implementation of monetary policy,
- Providing settlement services and ensuring the stability of the financial system,
- Treasury and government securities-related operations,
- International activities,
- Compilation of data, economic analyses, and research activities.[19]

Appendix 3: History of the Bank of Japan

The nation's central bank was established through the Bank of Japan Act and began operations on 10 October 1882. Like most modern Japanese institutions, it was founded after the Meiji Restoration. Prior to the Restoration, Japan's feudal fiefs all issued their own money, *hansatsu*, in an array of incompatible denominations. The New Currency Act of Meiji 4 (1871) did away with these and established the JPY as the new currency. The former *han* (fiefs) became prefectures and their mints became private chartered banks, which initially retained the right to print money. For a time, both the central government and these so-called national banks issued money. This ended when the BOJ was given a monopoly to control the supply of money and issued its first banknotes in 1885. In 1899, the former "national" banknotes were formally rendered obsolete.

The bank was reorganized on 1 May 1942 to comply with the Bank of Japan Act, which went into effect in February 1942. The act reflected the wartime situation: for example, Article 1 stated that the objectives of the bank were regulation of the currency, control and facilitation of credit and finance, and the maintenance and fostering of the credit system,

---

[19]Bank of Japan, http://www.boj.or.jp/en/, accessed 5 June 2022.

pursuant to national polity, in order that the general economic activities of the nation might adequately be enhanced.[20]

Except for a brief post-World War II hiatus when the occupying allies issued military currency and restructured the bank into a more independent entity, the BOJ has operated ever since. The 1942 legislation was amended several times after that war. An amendment in 1949 allowed the establishment of a policy board as the bank's highest decision-making body.

Despite a major 1997 rewrite of the Bank of Japan Act that intended to give the bank more independence, the BOJ has been criticized for lack of independence. A certain degree of dependence was enshrined in the act itself. Article 4 states: In recognition of the fact that currency and monetary control is a component of overall economic policy, the BOJ shall always maintain close contact with the government and exchange views sufficiently, so that its currency and monetary control and the basic stance of the government's economic policy shall be mutually harmonious.

In June 1997, the act was again amended with two key principles — independence and transparency. The revised act went into effect on 1 April 1998.

Appendix 4: The BOJ's Independence

The Bank of Japan Act states:

(1) The Bank of Japan's autonomy regarding currency and monetary control shall be respected. (Article 3, Paragraph 1).
(2) Due consideration shall be given to the autonomy of the Bank's business operations. (Article 5, Paragraph 2).
(3) To ensure the independence of the bank, members of the Policy Board, which is the bank's highest decision-making body, cannot be dismissed for holding opinions at variance with the government, and the government cannot order the bank to undertake any particular policy action or to conduct any particular business operation. (Article 14).

---

[20]National polity was the notion that all authority and privilege reside in the nation and the emperor. The national mobilization for war was heavily promoted through this notion of "national polity," and all citizens were pressured to fulfill their duty for national polity.

(4)   It is important that the bank's monetary policy be consistent with the government's basic economic policy framework, so it states that the bank shall "always maintain close contact with the government and exchange views sufficiently." (Article 4).

(5)   The Bank of Japan Act also allows representatives of the government to attend monetary policy meetings of the policy board, to give their views and submit proposals, or request that the board postpone a vote on monetary policy measures until the next meeting. (Article 19).

(6)   The government representatives have no votes in the monetary policy decisions, and the decisions are made only by a majority vote of the nine members of the policy board. (Article 19).[21]

Appendix 5: International Monetary Funds Code of Good Practices for Transparency in Monetary and Financial Policies for Central Banks

The International Monetary Fund (IMF) has developed a Code of Good Practices on Transparency in Monetary and Financial Policies. The code was developed in cooperation with the Bank for International Settlements, in consultation with central banks, financial agencies, relevant international and regional organizations, and academic experts. It was premised on four principles:

(1) Clarity of Roles, Responsibilities, and Objectives: The objectives of the central bank for monetary policy should be clearly defined, publicly disclosed, and written into law. The institutional relationship between monetary and fiscal policies should be clearly defined, as should any agency roles performed by the central bank on behalf of the government. For financial agencies, their objectives and institutional framework should be clearly defined, preferably in relevant legislation or regulation, and the role of oversight agencies with regard to payment systems should be publicly disclosed.

(2) Open Process for Formulating and Reporting Policy Decisions: Central banks should publicly disclose and explain the framework,

---

[21]Bank of Japan Act, Law No. 89 of 1998, https://liblawuw.libguides.com/c.php?g=1239338&p=9069990, accessed 5 June 2022.

instruments, and targets, if any, which are used to achieve objectives. The structure of their decision-making bodies should be publicly disclosed and their decisions communicated in a timely manner. Periodic public statements should be made on progress toward achieving monetary policy objectives. The conduct of financial policies by financial agencies should be transparent and compatible with confidentiality considerations and the need to preserve effectiveness. Periodic progress reports on the pursuance of policy objectives should be issued.

(3) Public Availability of Information on Policies: For central banks, information on monetary policy should be consistent with the IMF's standards for data dissemination and its balance sheet should be publicly available.[22] The central bank should establish and maintain public information services. Financial agencies should issue periodic public reports on major developments in the financial system, report aggregate data on a timely and regular basis, make texts of regulations and directives readily available to the public, and publicly disclose special protections, such as deposit insurance schemes and consumer protection arrangements.

(4) Accountability and Assurances of Integrity: Central bank officials should periodically appear before a designated public authority to explain the conduct and performance of their policy. The central bank should provide assurances of the integrity of operations and officials through the release of audited financial statements of its operations and the standards of conduct for its officials. The code suggested similar practices to hold officials of financial agencies accountable for their actions.

For Further Discussion

(1) Evaluate the risks and side effects of the BOJ's new monetary easing.
(2) When Japan's former Prime Minister Shinzo Abe suggested that the BOJ was a "government subsidiary" at a meeting in Oita, Japan, on 11 March 2022, he was referring to the BOJ's purchase of JGB through money market operations. Chinami Nishimura, the

---

[22]*Source*: "IMF, TRANSPARENCY AT THE IMF." IMF, July 2023, https://www.imf.org/en/About/Factsheets/Sheets/2023/Transparency-at-the-imf, accessed 21 July 2023.

secretary-general of Japan's leading opposition Constitutional Democratic Party was among those who criticized Abe's comment about the BOJ. Is the BOJ's independence defined as operational rather than absolute?

(3) What is modern monetary theory (MMT)? Explain the differences that exist between mainstream monetary theory and MMT. Does MMT theory work? It is said that Japan is an example of MMT. Do you agree?

(4) What is the significance of the JPY as a currency? Consider the position of JPY as a traded currency and a reserve currency when answering this question.

Appendix: Sales Record of Misawa's Cases through Harvard Business Publishing Online

(1) Currently, Misawa's 23 Cases are listed on Harvard Business Publishing Online (see Figure 1A). Visit Harvard Business Online under Misawa: https://hbsp.harvard.edu/search?N=&Nrpp=10&Ntt= MITSURU+MISAWA.

In 2021, I sold 5,214 copies of my cases through Harvard Business Publishing.

The total number of my cases sold in the past 15 years is now 46,924 copies as shown in Table 1A.

The big 50 users of my cases in 2021 were as in Table 2A. The users of my cases are from across the world.

(2) My recent case on Toshiba is the best seller at Harvard (see Figure 2A). The case is titled "The Toshiba Accounting Scandal: How Corporate Governance Failed." Through Harvard, I sold 1,483 copies of my Toshiba case in 2021.

The Toshiba case has been very popular for the last few years and ranked as the top 20 most popular cases at Harvard. For Toshiba's case, I sold 6,964 copies (2,032 + 2,075 + 1,374 + 1,483) in the past 4 years (2018–2021).

Figure 1A: Misawa's 21 Cases Listed on Harvard Business Publishing Online

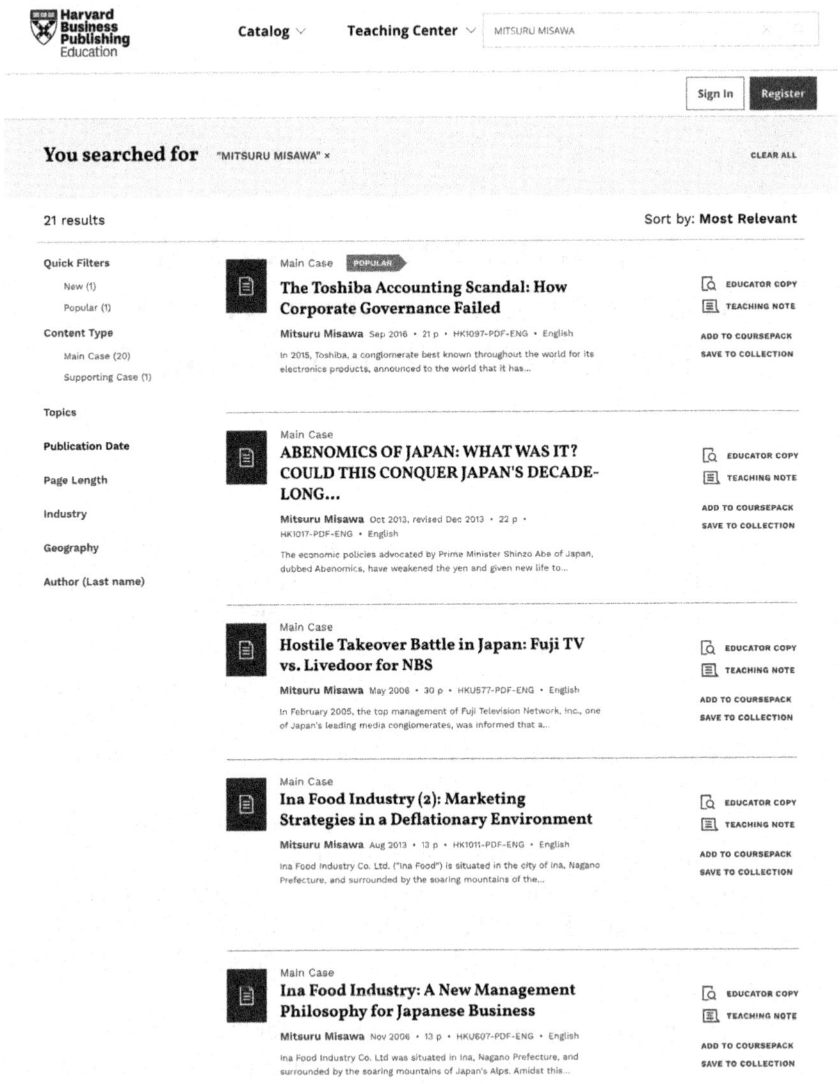

Figure 1A: *(Continued)*

Main Case

Interest-Rate Swap Offered by Sumitomo-Mitsui Bank: Was This for Hedging or...

Mitsuru Misawa Mar 2017 · 15 p · HK1105-PDF-ENG · English

Sumitomo-Mitsui Bank (the Bank) was found not to have breached its duty of explanation when an interest-rate swap agreement had been...

🔎 EDUCATOR COPY
📄 TEACHING NOTE

ADD TO COURSEPACK
SAVE TO COLLECTION

Main Case

Licensing Arrangement Or Joint Venture (4): An Ex Post Case Study Of Tokyo...

Misawa Mitsuru Nov 2012 · 20 p · HKU988-PDF-ENG · English

In the late 1970s, Walt Disney Corporation sought to expand its enterprise to Japan. Oriental Land Corp, which represented the Japanese...

🔎 EDUCATOR COPY
📄 TEACHING NOTE

ADD TO COURSEPACK
SAVE TO COLLECTION

Main Case

Livedoor: The Rise and Fall of a Market Maverick

Misawa Mitsuru Jun 2006 · 13 p · HKU579-PDF-ENG · English

Internet service firm Livedoor allegedly took advantage of loopholes in securities trading laws to swell the amount of assets held by the...

🔎 EDUCATOR COPY
📄 TEACHING NOTE

ADD TO COURSEPACK
SAVE TO COLLECTION

Main Case   NEW

Negative Interest Rates: The Bank of Japan Experience

Mitsuru Misawa Jun 2020 · 17 p · HK1235-PDF-ENG · English

Despite Prime Minister Shinzo Abe's new economic strategy, known as "Abenomics," being enacted in 2012, Japan's deflationary spiral...

🔎 EDUCATOR COPY
📄 TEACHING NOTE

ADD TO COURSEPACK
SAVE TO COLLECTION

Main Case

Nireco Co., Japan: Introduction of the Poison Pill

Mitsuru Misawa Oct 2006 · 26 p · HKU593-PDF-ENG · English

Japanese corporations faced the looming threat of hostile takeovers because of the rapid dissolution of cross-shareholdings that began in...

🔎 EDUCATOR COPY
📄 TEACHING NOTE

ADD TO COURSEPACK
SAVE TO COLLECTION

Quick Filters

New (1)

Popular (1)

Content Type

Main Case (20)

Supporting Case (1)

Topics

Publication Date

Page Length

Industry

Geography

Main Case

OSG Corporation: Risk Hedging Against Transaction Exposures

Mitsuru Misawa Dec 2006 · 22 p · HKU618-PDF-ENG · English

In Tokyo on Monday, April 24th, 2006, the U.S. dollar fell to a three-month low against the yen, carrying over its weakness from Friday's...

🔎 EDUCATOR COPY
📄 TEACHING NOTE

ADD TO COURSEPACK
SAVE TO COLLECTION

Main Case

Rogue Trader at Daiwa Bank (A): Management Responsibility Under Different...

Mitsuru Misawa Nov 2005 · 15 p · HKU442-PDF-ENG · English

In 1995, Sumio Abekawa, Daiwa Bank's president, received a letter on July 18 from Toshihide Iguchi, vice-president of the bank's New York...

🔎 EDUCATOR COPY
📄 TEACHING NOTE

ADD TO COURSEPACK
SAVE TO COLLECTION

Figure 1A: *(Continued)*

Author (Last name)

Supporting Case

Rogue Trader at Daiwa Bank (B): The Board Meeting on September 25th 1995 in...

Mitsuru Misawa Nov 2005 • 4 p • HKU444-PDF-ENG • English

An abstract is not available for this product.

EDUCATOR COPY
TEACHING NOTE
ADD TO COURSEPACK
SAVE TO COLLECTION

Main Case

Saizeriya and the Use of Foreign Currency Coupon Swaps: Was This for Hedging or...

Mitsuru Misawa Mar 2014 • 38 p • HK1037-PDF-ENG • English

Ever since Yasuhiko Shogaki took over Saizeriya Co., Ltd. (Saizeriya) in 1968, the restaurant had aimed to provide healthy and tasty...

EDUCATOR COPY
TEACHING NOTE
ADD TO COURSEPACK
SAVE TO COLLECTION

Main Case

Sales Tax Increase in 2014 Under Abenomics: The Japanese Government's Dilemma

Mitsuru Misawa Oct 2015 • 14 p • HK1073-PDF-ENG • English

On October 1, 2013 at a meeting of ruling party officials, Japanese Prime Minister Shinzo Abe said that he had decided to go ahead with a...

EDUCATOR COPY
TEACHING NOTE
ADD TO COURSEPACK
SAVE TO COLLECTION

Main Case

Softbank's New Strategy: The Largest LBO in Japan

Mitsuru Misawa Jan 2008 • 22 p • HKU793-PDF-ENG • English

On 17 March 2006, Japanese Internet company Softbank Corp announced that it had reached a final agreement with British cellular phone giant...

EDUCATOR COPY
TEACHING NOTE
ADD TO COURSEPACK
SAVE TO COLLECTION

Main Case

Tokyo Disneyland (3): New Pricing Policy Needed For Sluggish Demand

Mitsuru Misawa Nov 2012 • 17 p • HKU986-PDF-ENG • English

On 9 May 2005, Oriental Land Co, Ltd ("OL") announced changes in the company's top management. They were feeling the heat not only from the...

EDUCATOR COPY
TEACHING NOTE
ADD TO COURSEPACK
SAVE TO COLLECTION

Main Case

Tokyo Disneyland and the DisneySea Park: Corporate Governance and Differences...

Mitsuru Misawa Mar 2006 • 26 p • HKU568-PDF-ENG • English

In 1997, building on its earlier success with Tokyo Disneyland, Oriental Land Corp. Japan and the Walt Disney Co. discussed the possibility...

EDUCATOR COPY
TEACHING NOTE
ADD TO COURSEPACK
SAVE TO COLLECTION

Main Case

Tokyo Disneyland: Licensing vs. Joint Venture

Mitsuru Misawa Aug 2005 • 22 p • HKU420-PDF-ENG • English

Tokyo Disneyland was started as a result of a licensing agreement between Walt Disney (WD) of the United States and Oriental Land Corp....

EDUCATOR COPY
TEACHING NOTE
ADD TO COURSEPACK
SAVE TO COLLECTION

Figure 1A: *(Continued)*

Main Case

Toyota's New Business Model: Creating a Sustainable Future

Mitsuru Misawa Nov 2019 • 12 p • HK1206-PDF-ENG • English

Many companies study the management strategies of others, adapting and
learning from the experiences of large multinationals. But global...

EDUCATOR COPY

TEACHING NOTE

ADD TO COURSEPACK

SAVE TO COLLECTION

Quick Filters

New (1)

Popular (1)

Content Type

Main Case (20)

Supporting Case (1)

Main Case

World Co. Ltd, Japan: Why Go Private?

Mitsuru Misawa Jan 2008 • 19 p • HKU699-PDF-ENG • English

Early 2005 saw the first hostile takeover in Japan. Financed by foreign
capital, the takeover startled Japan's traditional business...

EDUCATOR COPY

TEACHING NOTE

ADD TO COURSEPACK

SAVE TO COLLECTION

Harvard Business Publishing

HIGHER EDUCATION

Contact Us

Copyright Permission

Help Center

In The News

Inspiring Minds

Partners

Privacy Policy

HARVARD BUSINESS PUBLISHING

About Us

Careers

Corporate Learning

Harvard Business Review

HBR Ascend

Trademark Policy

CONNECT

f Facebook

Twitter

in LinkedIn

YouTube

Help

TOP

Table 1A: Sales Record of My Cases in the Past 15 Years

Year	Copies
2007	2,060
2008	1,555
2009	1,895
2010	2,151
2011	1,492
2012	1,798
2013	2,575
2014	2,778
2015	4,085
2016	2,833
2017	4,093
2018	5,158
2019	4,607
2020	4,630
2021	5,214
Total	**46,924**

Table 2A: The Users of Misawa's Cases in 2021

1.	**University of Hong Kong (Hong Kong)**	**981**
2.	Indian Institute of Management (India)	429
3.	Monash University (Australia)	382
4.	International College of Management, Sydney (Australia)	270
5.	**IE Business School (Spain)**	**241**
6.	University of New South Wales (Australia)	212
7.	**Michigan State University (US)**	**196**
8.	Warwick Business School (UK)	170
9.	Narsee Monjee Institute of Management Studies (India)	160
10.	Holy Family University (US)	144
11.	California State University, Los Angeles, Irvine, and San Bernardino (US)	141
12.	**Bocconi University (Italy)**	**132**
13.	Fudan University (China)	105
14.	Nagoya University of Commerce & Business (NUCB) (Japan)	77
15.	American University of Beirut (Lebanon)	67

Table 2A: *(Continued)*

16. Hong Kong University of Science and Technology (China)	64
17. SP Jain School of Global Management — Dubai (United Arab Emirates)	59
18. Asian Institute of Management (Philippines)	57
19. **Hitotsubashi University (Japan)**	**54**
20. Universidad Del Pacifico (Peru)	54
21. **Kyoto University (Japan)**	**53**
22. Hofstra University (US)	47
23. University EAFIT (Colombia)	46
24. Fachhochschule Bonn-Rhein-Sieg (Germany)	40
25. CEIBS (China)	40
27. University of Lagos Business School (Nigeria)	33
28. University of Navarra (Spain)	31
29. School of Economics and Management, Tongi University (SEM) (China)	30
30. **University of Washington (US)**	**29**
31. National University of Singapore (Singapore)	29
32. **International University of Japan (Japan)**	**29**
33. Clark Atlanta University (US)	26
34. King Fahd University of Petroleum & Minerals (Saudi Arabia)	25
35. University of Manitoba (Canada)	24
36. Institute of Management Technology — Dubai (United Arab Emirates)	22
37. Nauyang Technological University (Singapore)	22
38. **Korea University (South Korea)**	**21**
39. Providence College (US)	21
40. Universidad Libero Americana (Mexico)	21
41. University of Virginia (US)	21
42. **George Washington University (US)**	**20**
43. Empire State University (US)	20
44. **New York University (US)**	**19**
45. University of Poritificia Comillas de Madrid (Spain)	18
46. **Penn State — Abington (US)**	**17**
47. Hamburg University of Technology (Germany)	17
48. Brandeis University (US)	16
49. Lahore University of Management Sciences (Pakistan)	16
50. Wake Forest University (US)	15
51. **Aoyama Gakuin University (Japan)**	**15**

(Continued)

Table 2A: *(Continued)*

52. Brigham Young University (US)	15
53. SDM Institute for Management and Development (India)	15
54. **Georgetown University (US)**	**14**
55. **Kyoto University (Japan)**	**14**
56. MBS Textbook Exchange, Inc. (US)	14
57. Universidad Panamericana (Mexico)	13
58. Capilano University (Canada)	12
59. Bentley University (US)	12
60. University of Delaware (US)	11
61. Universiti Utara Malaysia (Malaysia)	10
62. Universidad del Montevideo (Uruguay)	10
63. Western State College (US)	10
64. Xiamen University of Technology (China)	7
65. Universidade Catolica Portuguesa, Lisbon (Portugal)	5
66. University of Sydney (China)	5
67. Centre College (US)	4
68. University of Windsor (Canada)	4
69. National Taiwan Normal University (Taiwan)	3
70. Northeast Normal University (China)	3
71. University of Hygo (Japan)	3
72. Thammasat Business School (Thailand)	3
73. McGill University (Canada)	3
74. MacEwan University (Canada)	2
75. University Rafael Landivar (Guatemala)	2
76. Durham University Business School (UK)	2
77. Kansai Gaidai University (Japan)	1
78. IESA Venezuela (Venezuela)	1
79. University of Vienna (Austria)	1
80. University of the West Indies (Antigua and Barbuda)	1
81. University of Victoria (Canada)	1
82. The Elms School (US)	1
83. Queen's University Belfast (UK)	1
84. Hebrew University of Jerusalem (Israel)	1
85. Case Western Reserve University (US)	1
86. Providence College (US)	1
Total	**5,214**

Figure 2A:　Misawa's Toshiba Case, the Best Seller at Harvard

📄 Main Case　POPULAR

The Toshiba Accounting Scandal: How Corporate Governance Failed

Mitsuru Misawa

EDUCATOR COPY　　TEACHING NOTE　　SHARE

Accounting ethics, Crisis management, Accounting, Disclosure, Corporate governance, Transparency, Scandals

In 2015, Toshiba, a conglomerate best known throughout the world for its electronics products, announced to the world that it has overstated profits by 151.8 billion yen (US$1.2 billion) over a seven-year period. The conduct of Toshiba's management and employees left a deep stain on Japan that threw corporate culture and corporate governance practices into turmoil. This case presents a comprehensive overview of the Toshiba accounting scandal. It examines how the accounting irregularities in evidence at Toshiba spread from a relatively minor case of accounting misrepresentation to corporate-wide deception ingrained in the cultural fabric of the organization. The research highlights how issues of corporate culture can undermine even the most robust corporate governance strategies, and examines some of the challenges Toshiba faces in its attempts to recover from the biggest accounting scandal in contemporary Japanese history.

My other recent cases listed as follows were also selling well in 2021.

	Copies
(1) The Toshiba Accounting Scandal: How Corporate Governance Failed	1,483
(2) Negative Interest Rates: The Bank of Japan Experience	824
(3) Interest-Rate Swap Offered by Sumitomo Mitsui Banking Corporation: Was This for Hedging or Speculation?	810

(3) The past 15 years' record shows that top schools have been using my cases and the sales of my cases have been growing more and more popular worldwide now. The users in the US and foreign countries are shown in Table 3A.

Table 3A: Largest Users of Misawa's Cases in the Past 15 Years (2009–2021)

USA	Copies
1. **Harvard Business School (MBA)**	**1,453**
2. Rasmussen — Illinois (Online College)	1,010
3. **University of Washington**	**715**
4. **MIT**	**565**
5. **Northwestern University**	**479**
6. **Boston University**	**444**
7. California State University, Los Angeles and San Bernardino	411
8. **Shidler College of Business, University of Hawaii at Manoa**	**322**
9. **Michigan State University**	**266**
10. Holy Family University	300
11. Temple University	163
12. **USC**	**158**
13. Bethel University	138
14. **Wharton, University of Pennsylvania**	**110**
15. Nova Southeastern University	107
16. College of William and Mary	102
17. Wake Forest University	89
18. Conny-Brooklyn	88
19. **New York University**	**86**
20. **University of North Carolina — Chapel Hills**	**85**
21. **University of Pittsburgh**	**80**
22. **Cornell University**	**78**
23. Tulane University	78
24. Willamette University	72
25. Hofstra University	64
25. **George Washington University**	**62**

Table 3A: *(Continued)*

26. University of Miami	62
27. University of Texas at San Antonio	58
28. **Georgetown University**	**55**
29. **Penn State**	**54**
30. Bentley	48
31. Empire State College	44
32. Clark Atlanta University	40
33. University of Minnesota	35
34. McMaster University	35
35. **Yale University**	**34**
36. Niagara University	27
37. George Mason University	27
38. Grand Valley State University	25
39. University of Kentucky	24
40. Providence College	22
41. University of Virginia	21
42. Adelphi University	21
43. Brandeis University	20
44. **Columbia University**	**19**
45. Hood College B&N Bookstore #029	19
46. **University of California — Irvine**	**17**
47. Business School Sao Paulo (BCP)	17
48. Massachusetts College of Liberal Arts	17
49. Western Michigan University	16
50. Brigham Young University	15
51. University of New Hampshire	14
52. Southern University and A&M College	14
53. Thomas College	11
54. University of Delaware	11
55. Western State College	10
56. University of Massachusetts	10
57. Western Illinois University	8
58. California State University — Los Angeles	8

(Continued)

Table 3A: *(Continued)*

59. **Yale University**	7
60. University of Kansas	6
61. Rutgers University	6
62. University of Connecticut	6
63. Loyola University — Chicago	6
64. Centre College	4
65. **University of Michigan**	**4**
66. Marshall University	3
67. Grand Valley State University	2
68. Chatham College	2
69. Oliver Wyman	2
70. **Boston College**	**2**
71. Marshall University	2
72. University of San Francisco	2
73. University of South Florida	1
74. Juniata College	2
75. Arkansas Northeastern College	1
76. Touro University Worldwide	1
77. The Elms School	1
78. Case Western Reserve University	1
Foreign	**Copies**
1. Mownash University (Australia)	2,658
(The 69th university in the world according to the QS World University Ranking)	
2. **University of Hong Kong (Hong Kong)**	**1,577**
3. Indian Institute of Management — Bangalore and Calcutta (India)	1,487
4. SP Jain School of Global Management — Dubai (United Arab Emirates)	1,132
5. **Graduate School of Management, GLOBIS (Japan)**	**932**
(As the largest and fastest-growing business school in *Japan, ranked* first in student satisfaction among *Japanese* MBA schools by *Nikkei Career Magazine*)	
6. **SDA Bacconi School of Management (Italy)**	**698**
(Ranked 5th MBA in Europe and 15th in the world by the *Financial Times*)	

Table 3A: *(Continued)*

7.	University of New South Wales (Australia)	634
8.	**IE Business School (Spain)**	**617**
9.	**Instituto De Empresa, Business (Spain)**	**596**
	(*Financial Times*, European Business School Ranking, 1st in Europe)	
10.	**University of Melbourne (Australia)**	**424**
11.	**Bocconi University (Italy)**	**347**
12.	**Concordia University (Canada)**	**337**
	(The university's John Molson School of Business is consistently ranked among the top 10 Canadian business schools, and within the top 100 worldwide)	
13.	Lahore University of Management Sciences (Pakistan)	335
14.	SP Jain Institute of Management and Research (SPJIMR) (India)	316
15.	International College of Management, Sydney (Australia)	316
16.	Narsee Monjee Institute of Management Studies (India)	315
	(Leading business school ranked 4th best B School in India)	
17.	Asian Institute of Management, Makati City (Philippines)	287
18.	**National University of Singapore (Singapore)**	**264**
	(The *Financial Times* placed NUS at 26th in the world and second in Asia. Yale NUS College is a liberal arts college in Singapore, opened in August 2013, as a joint project of Yale University and NUS)	
19.	Xavier Labour Relations Institute (XLRI) (India)	262
20.	University Ulara Malaysia (Malaysia)	246
21.	**Hitotsubashi University (Japan)**	**240**
22.	Universidad EAFIT (Columbia)	233
	(Established in partnership with Harvard Business School and uses the Harvard Business School case study teaching methodology. One of the few business schools in Asia to be internationally accredited with the AACSB)	
23.	**Waseda University (Japan)**	**207**
24.	**University of Queensland Business School (Australia)**	**206**
	(The Financial placed NUS at 26th in the world and second in Asia. Yale NUS College is a liberal arts college in Singapore, opened in August 2013, as a joint project of Yale University and NUS)	

(Continued)

Table 3A: (*Continued*)

25.	International University of Japan (Japan)	**211**
26.	Warwick Business School (UK)	170
27.	Hong Kong University of Science and Technology (China)	166
28.	**Kyoto University (Japan)**	**164**
29.	Narsee Monjee Institute of Management Studies (India)	160
30.	AUDENCIA Nantes School of Management (France)	158
31.	Nirma University (India)	129
32.	University of Haifa (Israel)	126
33.	Nagoya University of Commerce & Business (NUCB) (Japan)	121
34.	TiasNimbas Business School (Netherlands)	116
35.	**Lund University (Sweden)**	**116**
	(As one of the most renowned institutions of higher learning in the Nordic countries, ranked 1st among comprehensive universities in Scandinavia and 123rd in the world by the *Financial Times* Rankings)	
36.	University College Dublin (UCD) College of Business & Law (Ireland)	112
37.	Fudan University (China)	105
38.	University of Windsor (Canada)	105
39.	King's Business School (UK)	102
40.	Chulalongkorn University (Thailand)	100
41.	Chinese University of Hong Kong (China)	90
42.	**University of Oxford (UK)**	**85**
43.	KAIST (Korea Advanced Institute of Science and Technology) (North Korea)	84
44.	Educomp Raffles Higher Education (India)	80
45.	University of Zurich — Executive MBA (Switzerland)	75
46.	University of Zurich — Executive MBA (Switzerland)	75
47.	The University of Nottingham Ningbo China (China)	70
48.	American University of Beirut (Lebanon)	67
49.	Capilano University (Canada)	67
50.	**Kyoto University (Japan)**	**67**
51.	Concordia University (Canada)	66
52.	Universidad Panamericana (Mexico)	65
53.	University of Toronto (Canada)	64

Table 3A: *(Continued)*

54.	Bogazici University (Turkey)	62
55.	WHU — Otto Beisheim School of Management (Germany)	60
56.	IESEG School of Management (France)	56
57.	Universidad Del Pacifico (Peru)	54
58.	Temple University (Singapore)	50
59.	School of Economics and Management, Tongi University (SEM) (China)	49
60.	Nanyang Technological University (Singapore)	46
61.	City University of Hong Kong (Hong Kong)	45
62.	Carleton University (Canada)	43
63.	Luiss Business School of Rome (Italy)	42
64.	Fachhochschule Bonn-Rhein-Sieg (Germany)	40
65.	PUC Rio UNIVERSITY (Brazil)	36
66.	FGV-EAESP (Brazil)	35
67.	FGV-EAESP (Brazil)	35
68.	University of Manitoba (Canada)	34
69.	University of Lagos Business School (Nigeria)	33
70.	International Management Institute — New Delhi (IMI) (India)	32
71.	University of Navarra (Spain)	31
72.	EDHEC — Business School (France)	31
73.	**Keio University (Japan)**	**30**
74.	The University of Edinburgh Business School (UK)	28
75.	National Taiwan University of Science and Technology (Taiwan)	27
76.	University of Lagos Business School (Nigeria)	26
77.	Sasin Graduate Institute of Business Administration (Thailand)	25
78.	King Fahd University of Petroleum & Minerals (Saudi Arabia)	25
79.	**Korea University (South Korea)**	**25**
80.	Grow Talent Company (India)	23
81.	Wilfrid Laurier University (Canada)	21
82.	Universidad Rafael Landivar (URL) (Guatemala)	22
83.	Institute of Management Technology — Dubai (United Arab Emirates)	22
84.	Universidad Libero Americana (Mexico)	21
85.	NIDA — National Institute of Development Administration (Thailand)	20
86.	Suresh Gyan Vihar University (India)	20

(Continued)

Table 3A: *(Continued)*

87. Peking University HSBC School of Business (China)	20
88. **Nagoya University (Japan)**	**20**
89. NIDA — National Institute of Development Administration (Thailand)	20
90. Auckland University of Technology (AUT) (New Zealand)	19
91. Karachi School for Business and Leadership (KSBL) (Pakistan)	19
92. **Doshisha University (Japan)**	**18**
93. University of Poritificia Comillas de Madrid (Spain)	18
94. Hamburg University of Technology (Germany)	17
95. Wilfrid Laurier University (Canada)	16
96. ITESM Tecnologico de Monterrey (Guadalajara) (Mexico)	16
97. Bond University (Australia)	16
98. Queen's University (Canada)	16
99. Aalen University (Germany)	15
100. **Aoyama Gakuin University (Japan)**	**15**
101. SDM Institute for Mgt and Development (India)	15
102. National Tsing Hua University (Taiwan)	14
103. Pontificia Universidad Javeriana (Colombia)	14
104. Universidad de Chile (Chile)	11
105. National Taiwan Normal University (Taiwan)	11
106. NITIE — National Institute of Industrial Engineering (India)	10
107. Technishe Hochschule Georg (Germany)	10
108. Universiti Utara Malaysia (Malaysia)	10
109. Northeast Normal University (China)	9
110. Singapore Management University (Singapore)	8
111. Institute of Management Technology — Nagpur (IMT) (India)	7
112. Xiamen University of Technology (China)	7
113. Shanghai International Studies University (China)	6
114. IESA Venezuela (Venezuela)	6
115. John F. Kennedy School of Government (Mexico)	6
116. Western University (Canada)	6
117. University of Sheffield (UK)	6
118. McGill University (Canada)	6
119. International University of Japan (Japan)	5
120. IFIM Business School (India)	5

Table 3A: *(Continued)*

121.	Universidade Catolica Portuguesa, Lisbon (Portugal)	5
122.	University of Sydney (China)	5
123.	Hochschule Fresenius (Germany)	4
124.	Fairleigh Dickinson University (Canada)	4
125.	CETYS Universidad (Mexico)	4
126.	Taylor's University (Malaysia)	3
127.	VietSeeds Foundation (Vietnam)	3
128.	National Taiwan Normal University (Taiwan)	3
129.	Thammasat Business School (Thailand)	3
130.	University of Hygo (Japan)	3
131.	McGill University (Canada)	3
132.	MacEwan University (Canada)	2
133.	University of Prince Edward Island (Canada)	2
134.	University Gadjah Mada (Indonesia)	2
135.	Durham University Business School (UK)	1
136.	Kansai Gaidai University (Japan)	1
137.	IESA Venezuela (Venezuela)	1
138.	University of Vienna (Austria)	1
139.	University of the West Indies (Antigua and Barbuda)	1
140.	University of Victoria (Canada)	1
141.	Queen's University Belfast (UK)	1
142.	Hebrew University of Jerusalem (Israel)	1
143.	Case Western Reserve University (US)	1
144.	Providence College (US)	1
145.	Clark University (Canada)	1
146.	De Montfort University (UK)	1
147.	University of Pelita Harapan (Indonesia)	1
148.	University Finis Terrae (Chile)	1
149.	Xiamen University (Malaysia)	1
150.	FH Munster University for Applied Science (Germany)	1
151.	LG Economic Research Institute (Canada)	1
152.	Kobe University (Japan)	1
153.	University of Tokyo (Japan)	1
154.	Kansai Gaidai University (Japan)	1

(Continued)

Table 3A: (*Continued*)

155. Universidad de Lima (Peru)	1
156. European (Spain)	1
157. Sasin Graduate Institute of Business Administration (Thailand)	1
158. Liberty University (Canada)	1
159. Nottingham University Business School (UK)	1
160. Thammasat Business School (Thailand)	1
Companies	
1. International Professional Managers Association (IPMA) (UK)	151
2. Stormont Consulting Firm (US)	23
3. Boston Consulting Group International (US)	**21**
4. Bain & Company, Inc. (US)	**16**
5. Nichibei Kaiwa Gakuin (Japan)	15
6. MBS Textbook Exchange, Inc. (US)	14
7. Management Association of Japan (Japan)	10
8. Goldman Sachs & Co. (US)	**5**
9. Content Works, Inc. (Japan)	1

(4) Sales records for top 10 cases in 2021 are shown in Table 4A.
Cases on Toshiba, BOJ, Sumitomo Mitsui Bank, Saizeria, and Tokyo
Disneyland are very popular.
(5) Sales records of my cases by country in 2021 are shown in Table 5A.

Table 4A: Sales Records of Misawa's Cases in 2021

Case Titles	Copies
1. The Toshiba Accounting Scandal: How Corporate Governance Failed	1,483
2. Negative Interest Rates: The Bank of Japan Experience	824
3. Interest-Rate Swap Offered by Sumitomo Mitsui Banking Corporation: Was This for Hedging or Speculation?	810
4. Rethinking Saizeria's Currency Hedging Strategy	365
5. OSG Corporation: Risk Hedging against Transaction	329
6. Tokyo Disneyland and the DisneySea Park: Corporate Governance and Differences in Capital Budgeting Concepts and Methods between American and Japanese Companies	298
7. Abenomics of Japan: What Was It? Could This Conquer Japan's Decade-Long Deflation?	284
8. Saizeriya and the Use of Foreign Currency Coupon Swaps: Was This for Hedging or Speculation?	207
9. Toyota's New Business Model: Creating a Sustainable Future	178
10. Ina Food Industry: A New Management Philosophy for Japanese Businesses	107
11. A Rogue Trader at Daiwa Bank (A): Management Responsibility Under Different Jurisprudential Systems, Practices, and Cultures	107
12. Licensing Arrangement or Joint Venture (4): An *Ex Post* Case Study of Tokyo Disneyland	87
13. Livedoor: The Rise and Fall of a Market Maverick	45
14. Softbank's New Strategy: The Largest LBO in Japan	35
15. A Rogue Trader at Daiwa Bank (B): The Board Meeting on September 25th, 1995 in Japan	27
16. Hostile Takeover Battle in Japan: Fuji TV vs. Livedoor for NBS	20
17. Sales Tax Increase in 2014 Under Abenomics: The Japanese Government's Dilemma	4
18. Tokyo Disneyland: Licensing vs. Joint Venture	3
19. Ina Food Industry (2): Marketing Strategies in a Deflationary Environment	1
Total	**5,214**

Table 5A: Sales Record of Misawa's Cases by Country in 2021

Year	Copies
1. Hong Kong	981
2. Australia	864
3. USA	802
4. India	444
5. China	414
6. Spain	291
7. Japan	246
8. UK	173
9. Italy	132
10. United Arab Emirates	81
11. Lebanon	67
12. Germany	57
13. Philippines	57
14. Peru	54
15. Singapore	51
16. Colombia	46
17. Canada	46
18. Mexico	35
19. Nigeria	33
20. Saudi Arabia	25
21. South Korea	21
22. Pakistan	16
23. Malaysia	10
24. Uruguay	10
25. Portugal	5
26. Taiwan	3
27. Thailand	3
28. Guatemala	2
29. Venezuela	1
30. Austria	1
31. Vietnam	1
32. Israel	1
33. Anfigua and Babunda	1
34. Others	235
Total	**5,214**

Index

Printed in the United States
by Baker & Taylor Publisher Services